Max Stafford-Clark

Educated at Trinity College, Dublin, Max Stafford-Clark co-founded Joint Stock Theatre Group in 1974 following his Artistic Directorship of the Traverse Theatre, Edinburgh. From 1979 to 1993 he was Artistic Director of the Royal Court Theatre, London. In 1993 he founded the touring company, Out of Joint.

His work as a director has overwhelmingly been with new writing, and he has commissioned and directed first productions by many leading writers, including Sue Townsend, Stephen Jeffreys, Timberlake Wertenb   oastian Barry, April de   gelis, Mark Ravenhill, Andrea l   Robin Soans, Alistair   ton, Stella Feehily, Sebastian   David Hare and   urchill. In addition he has dir   lassic texts inclu   S agu   *The Recruiting Officer* an   *Lear* for the Roya   *A Jovi* *The Wives' Excuse*   e *Country Wife* for   yal S   Company; and *T*   *of Mode*, *She S*   *Conqu* *Sisters* and *Macbe*   ut of Joint. He di   David l *Breath of Life* f   ley Theatre Com   n 2003, *Overwhelming* f   York's Roundabo   tre in 200

Academic cre   ude an honorar   orate from Brookes Univ   d Visiting Profes   ps at the Un   s of Hertfordsh   rwick and York. His   er books are *Let   to George* and *T*   *Stock*.

Maeve McKeown

Maeve McKeown is a theatre administrator, education practitioner and playwright. She was Administrator and Education Manager at Out of Joint Theatre Company, where she authored several education resource packs. She has also worked for Stephen Jeffreys' Playwriting Masterclass, UCL's Bloomsbury Theatre and as a freelance workshop leader. Her short plays have been produced by the National Youth Theatre and Soho Theatre. She is currently studying for a PhD in Political Philosophy at University College London.

Timberlake Wertenbaker

Timberlake Wertenbaker grew up in the Basque Country, in south-west France.

Her plays include *Case to Answer* (Soho Poly); *New Anatomies* (ICA); *Abel's Sister* (Royal Court); *The Grace of Mary Traverse* (Royal Court), winner of the Plays and Players' Award for Most Promising Playwright; *Our Country's Good* (Royal Court and Broadway), winner of the Olivier Award for Play of the Year, the New York Drama Critics' Circle Award for Best New Foreign Play, and nominated for a Tony Award; *The Love of the Nightingale* (Royal Shakespeare Company), winner of the Eileen Anderson Central TV Drama Award; *Three Birds Alighting on a Field* (Royal Court), winner of the Susan Smith Blackburn Award, the Writers' Guild Award and the London Critics' Circle Award; *The Break of Day* (Royal Court and on tour); *After Darwin* (Hampstead Theatre); *The Ash Girl* (Birmingham Rep); *Credible Witness* (Royal Court); *Galileo's Daughter* (Peter Hall Company at the Theatre Royal Bath); *Arden City* (National Theatre Connections Scheme) and *The Line* (Arcola Theatre).

Her translations and adaptations include Marivaux's *False Admissions*; *Successful Strategies* (Shared Experience); *La Dispute* (BBC Radio); Maurice Maeterlinck's *Pelleas and Melisande*; Ariane Mnouchkine's *Mephisto* (Royal Shakespeare Company); Eduardo de Filippo's *Filumena* (Peter Hall Company at the Piccadilly Theatre); Jean Anouilh's *Wild Orchids* (Chichester Festival Theatre); Sophocles' *Oedipus Tyrannos*, *Oedipus at Kolonos* and *Antigone* (Royal Shakespeare Company); Euripides' *Hecuba* (ACT, San Francisco); Gabriela Preissova's *Jenufa* (Natural Perspective Theatre Company with the Arcola Theatre); *The H. File* (from the novel by Ismail Kadare, BBC Radio 3); Euripides' *Hippolytus* (Riverside Studios and on tour); Racine's *Phedre* (Stratford Ontario Shakespeare Festival and ACT, San Francisco) and Sophocles' *Elektra* (Getty).

Opera and film work includes *The Love of the Nightingale* (composer Richard Mills, Perth Festival and on tour); *The Children* (directed by Tony Palmer) and *Do Not Disturb* (BBC2 Films). Original radio plays include *Dianeira*; *Divine Intervention*; *Scenes of Seduction* and *What is the Custom of Your Grief?*

Timberlake received an honorary doctorate from the Open University and was the Royden B. Davis Visiting Professor of Drama at Georgetown University in 2005–06. She is a fellow of the Royal Society of Literature and a member of PEN.

TIMBERLAKE WERTENBAKER'S

Our Country's Good

A study-guide by

Max Stafford-Clark
with Maeve McKeown

with photos by John Haynes

NICK HERN BOOKS
London
www.nickhernbooks.co.uk

A Nick Hern Book

Timberlake Wertenbaker's Our Country's Good – Page to Stage
first published in Great Britain in 2010
as a paperback original by Nick Hern Books Limited,
The Glasshouse, 49a Goldhawk Road, London W12 8QP

Reprinted 2012

Cover photograph by John Haynes:
Jude Akuwidike in the original Royal Court production of
Our Country's Good, 1988
Cover design by www.energydesignstudio.com

Typeset by Nick Hern Books, London
Printed and bound in Great Britain by
Mimeo Ltd, Huntingdon, Cambridgeshire PE29 6XX

A CIP catalogue record for this book is available
from the British Library

ISBN 978 1 84842 043 4

Contents

Acknowledgements

The authors and publisher gratefully acknowledge permission to quote from *The Fatal Shore* by Robert Hughes, published by Vintage Books, a division of Random House; *Our Country's Good* by Timberlake Wertenbaker, 2006 edition, published by Methuen Drama, an imprint of A&C Black Publishers Ltd; and *The Playmaker* by Thomas Keneally, published by Hodder and Stoughton Ltd.

With thanks to John Haynes for the use of his photographs of the original production.

Introduction

In 1787, eleven ships sailed from Britain to Botany Bay in the newly 'discovered' territory of Australia. The First Fleet carried a cargo of convicts and Royal Navy Officers, on course to establish a penal colony in New South Wales. In 1789, the convicts were allowed to put on a play – *The Recruiting Officer* by George Farquhar. *Our Country's Good* tells the story of this production from initial idea to opening night. The convict production faces obstacles at every level; from the vehement opposition of Major Robbie Ross, to the possibility that one of the female leads may be hanged. The eventual triumph of the play, and the journey on which it takes the brutalised convicts, is a powerful affirmation of the redemptive qualities of culture and education. *Our Country's Good* is one of the classic plays of the late twentieth century. It is regularly performed in professional theatres and studied in schools and universities.

*

The previous volumes in the Page to Stage series have considered Ibsen's *A Doll's House* and Chekhov's *Three Sisters*. These plays were written in the nineteenth and early twentieth centuries. By contrast *Our Country's Good* is a modern play first performed in 1988, so we have had direct access to the people who created it. I was the director of the company that first performed *Our Country's Good*. And Timberlake Wertenbaker, who wrote the play, kindly agreed to be interviewed for this book. We were also able to interview Linda Bassett, a member of the original company who performed the play at the Royal Court Theatre, London, and two members of the cast who staged the ten-year-anniversary revival in 1998, Sally Rogers and Ian Redford.

The first section of this book explains how the play came into being: based on Thomas Keneally's novel, *The Playmaker*, it was workshopped for two weeks at the Royal Court Theatre in April 1988 and performed later that year. This section also introduces the themes of the play – the treatment of convicted criminals, education, redemption and the power of theatre to effect change in people's lives. This is followed by a scene-by-scene synopsis of *Our Country's Good* and a synopsis of George Farquhar's *The Recruiting Officer*. There are also some notes as to how *The Recruiting Officer* is used throughout *Our Country's Good* to reflect the convicts' situations.

The second half of this book aims to delve a little deeper into how to approach the text of *Our Country's Good*. Each of the characters from the play is considered. Almost all of the characters in *Our Country's Good* are based on real historical figures and so it is important to have some understanding of their real-life stories. These notes are combined with what is written about the characters in both *Our Country's Good* and *The Playmaker*. There are two case studies: one of the Provost Marshal of Sydney, Harry Brewer, the other of the condemned convict Liz Morden, both based on the invaluable material from the interviews with cast members.

The section 'Rehearsing the Play' fleshes out the historical context in which *Our Country's Good* is set. Of course, this is not an attempt to write a history book, but an introduction to some of the key events and circumstances that affect the characters in *Our Country's Good*. Research was a large part of the rehearsal process for the play, as were my particular rehearsal techniques, which include actioning (finding the underlying intention in each line of a script), the importance of status in understanding the dynamics of a scene, and the use of cards to explore both status and intensity of feeling, which Stanislavsky would call the specific of the scene.

The final section, 'Staging the Play', approaches the design of a production of *Our Country's Good*. Firstly, there are some notes on the design of my own two productions of the play and then a scene-by-scene breakdown of the technical requirements for staging it.

Of course, every director, every actor, every student, will have their own ideas as to how to stage this powerful and evocative play. This book is in no way designed to be prescriptive. Rather, I hope it will shed some light on the complex and brilliant *Our Country's Good*, providing a way in, rather than a closed door.

Thanks to the following people whose contributions have been invaluable in the writing of this book. First of all, Gillian King, who wrote the education workpack for the 1998 Out of Joint production of *Our Country's Good* at the Young Vic; this workpack was instrumental in guiding this project. Also thanks to all those who agreed to be interviewed: Timberlake Wertenbaker, Linda Bassett, Sally Rogers and Ian Redford. And of course the publishers Nick Hern Books for all their help and support.

I wrote the first draft of the book over Christmas 2008, drawing on Gillian King's original workpack. Iain Sinclair, my Australian assistant on *The Convict's Opera*, contributed information about Aboriginal people. Maeve McKeown then embarked on redrafting of this version during the spring of 2009. This final version was edited by Nick Hern.

Max Stafford-Clark

Jim Broadbent (as Harry Brewer) takes Alphonsia Emmanuel (as Duckling Smith) for a boat trip around Sydney Cove in Act One, Scene Seven: 'Harry and Duckling Go Rowing'.

Writing 'Our Country's Good'

Timberlake Wertenbaker grew up in the Basque country, attending various schools in Europe and the USA. She studied Ancient Greek and Philosophy at university, subjects which would inform much of her future writing. After trying her hand at journalism she discovered a talent for playwriting when she was teaching French in Greece. This was after the military junta had burnt down all the libraries on the Greek islands, so a local teacher asked her to write some plays for the children, as they had no books to read.

Timberlake wrote a couple of other plays which were produced on the island and later sent them to the Soho Poly Theatre in London, where the Artistic Director Verity Bargate spotted her work. She was given a commission to write a play, which led to further commissions at the Royal Court Theatre. She then held the post of Writer in Residence at the Royal Court from 1984 to 1985. In her 1985 play *The Grace of Mary Traverse*, directed by Danny Boyle, she demonstrated a propensity for writing about the eighteenth century that I greatly admired.

THE IDEA

I was Artistic Director at the Royal Court from 1979 to 1993. In 1987, while searching for a candidate for the Royal Court's bi-annual production of a classic play, I came across Thomas Keneally's fascinating novel *The Playmaker*. Set in the nascent Australian colony, *The Playmaker* concerns the true story of an amateur convict production of George Farquhar's 1706 play *The Recruiting Officer*, performed for King George III's birthday on 4 June 1789.

The Playmaker tells the stories of several characters that sailed to Sydney in the First Fleet. At the centre of the novel is Lieutenant Ralph Clark – a young marine officer, desperate for promotion and plagued by homesickness. He directs the production of Farquhar's play and falls in love with one of the quieter female convicts, Mary Brenham. Ralph's friend, Harry Brewer, is the Provost Marshal in Sydney. Before securing this post, Harry had been the oldest midshipman in the Navy, a post usually held by children and teenagers, and is ridiculed by many of the senior officers. He is an alcoholic, tortured by visions of people he has hanged, and is embroiled in a complex relationship with Duckling, a young female convict. His Excellency Governor Arthur Phillip tries to govern the new colony in a humane and liberal way. A solitary figure in the novel, his conflicts with more conservative officers, including Major Robbie Ross, and his ambiguous relationship with the Aborigine, Arabanoo, are also explored.

I began re-reading *The Recruiting Officer* and the idea came to me to revive this classic Restoration comedy in rep with a commissioned adaptation of *The Playmaker*. I approached Timberlake about this project and she was very keen. She knew straight away that she wanted to write about the humanising power of theatre. My previous theatre company, Joint Stock, followed a particular working method. We would have a three-to-four-week workshop with a writer and a group of actors, where we researched a book or a theme. Then there would be a nine-to-ten-week gap when the writer would write the play. A more conventional rehearsal period would follow, in which the play could be redrafted and eventually staged. We agreed to work using this method, but after the two-week workshop for *Our Country's Good*, I would rehearse *The Recruiting Officer* with the same company of actors for five weeks, and when *The Recruiting Officer* opened, the actors would do four performances a week and rehearse Timberlake's play at the same time.

THE WORKSHOP

As we were discussing the project, however, Timberlake was struck by personal tragedy. Her partner John Price died suddenly and she didn't feel able to carry on. I coaxed her to participate in the workshop and assured her there was no pressure to produce a play, since *The Recruiting Officer* was in any case scheduled for rehearsal.

In April 1988 we began the two-week workshop with myself, Timberlake and eleven actors. This was mainly a research period, during which the actors read large chunks of Robert Hughes's remarkable study of early Australian history, *The Fatal Shore*. We immersed ourselves in eighteenth-century British and Australian history, using sources such as Lieutenant Ralph Clark's diaries from the Library of Australian History in Sydney, Roy Porter's *English Society in the Eighteenth Century* and Henry Mayhew's classic Victorian study of *London Labour and the London Poor*.

Timberlake brought a lot of her own research and experience to the room. She read all the novels and plays of the period, and studied the slang of the time – so-called 'canting' language. This is used throughout *Our Country's Good* as the convicts' native tongue. She was also particularly interested in education, and how it could reform people. She brought to my attention a study by R. Rosenthal and L. Jacobson called *Pygmalion in the Classroom*, which sought to prove the theory that if you *treat* people as intelligent, they *become* intelligent. This study is quoted at the front of the playtext, and Timberlake believes it is crucial to understanding the play. The themes of education, redemption and equality appear throughout *Our Country's Good*.

Part of the purpose of the workshop process is to encourage the actors to be direct participants in shaping the play. Each of them therefore had to do their own research on the themes of the story. Linda Bassett, who would play Liz Morden, and Alphonsia Emmanuel, who would play Duckling, got in touch with Clean Break, a theatre company who work with women affected by the criminal justice system. They interviewed a woman called Josie, who had spent her life in and out of prison and had been betrayed by her father at the age of twelve (see p. 61). Timberlake was particularly struck by this woman's story, and the way in which the two actresses recounted it to the group. This helped towards writing the character of Liz Morden in *Our Country's Good*.

As part of the same process, I sent the actor Nick Dunning, who was to play the convict Sideway and the officer Davy Collins, on a walk from London Bridge to the Drury Lane Theatre armed only with a map of eighteenth-century London. He was only able to navigate his way by 'seeing' the buildings and streets on the map rather than those he actually saw, and had to share his experience with the company.

Over the course of the two-week workshop we played a series of games and improvisation exercises based on the research material. One memorable improvisation played out over a whole day. In the morning all the actors were offered a deck of playing cards and asked to pick one at random. Whoever picked the Jack was the thief, and for the rest of the day had to recruit a look-out, and together steal as much as possible from the others without being detected. It led to considerable paranoia!

One of Timberlake's central concerns was the brutality of the relationship between the officers and the convicts in Sydney. 'What interests me,' she says, 'is what it means to be human at the extremes of humanity – so both the low extremes (cruelty) and high extremes (of surviving it and being redeemed). It's that question of 'What does it mean to be human?' – particularly now, having gone through the twentieth century, which has seen quite a bit of inhumanity.'

*

This prompted another improvisation using a pack of cards, designed to explore the brutality on board the convict ships. Each of the actors was dealt a card: two cards in a black suit signified they were guards; the higher the value of the card, the greater the disciplinarian they were. The rest of the actors were convicts, and the lower the cards they received, the more subservient they were. Once separated into these two groups, however, the degree of a guard's severity or a convict's resistance was kept secret. The guards were then given rolled-up newspapers, which made good weapons because you can hit someone quite hard with them, and make a lovely sound, without anyone getting hurt. Some of actors were very shrewd. Linda Bassett and Alphonsia Emmanuel, for example, cast as convicts, clocked early on that the guard being played by Mark Lambert probably had a high card, and steered clear of him, looking at the floor and behaving in a deferential manner, irrespective of their 'disobedience' ranking. On the other hand, Mossie Smith, who was to play Dabby Bryant, thought that Mark had only drawn a 2 or a 3, so went about farting at him, cheeking him and flashing at him at every opportunity. Unfortunately for Mossie, Mark had a 9, and he absolutely whacked her – she was squeaking with pain!

Another card-improvisation sought to uncover how good the convicts might have been as actors. I asked Mark Lambert, Mossie Smith and Lesley Sharp, who was to play Mary Brenham, to pick a card at random – the value on the card determining their theatrical ability. They had to work on a scene from *The Recruiting Officer*. Lesley drew a 2, and was therefore a hopelessly incompetent director; Mark got an 8 (quite a good actor), and his partner Mossie a 5: an untalented but enthusiastic actress. The resulting performance hit the heights (and depths) of tragi-comedy!

Although Timberlake didn't take much improvised material directly from the workshop to the page, improvisations like these certainly helped to form the play, as she herself explains: 'This is what you take and don't take from a workshop: in the scene where Major Ross is tormenting the actors in the second act, what came across in the improvisations was how, when you're being brutalised, you make yourself invisible, you cower, you go very quiet. So I used that.'

In fact, there was only one improvisation that Timberlake directly transferred from the workshop, into what become Act Two, Scene Six of *Our Country's Good*, entitled 'The Science of Hanging'. We had done some research into Albert Pierrepoint, one of the the last hangmen in Britain, which I found fascinating. Timberlake wasn't very interested, but I insisted on trying out an improvisation based on the grim methodology of hanging. This exercise involved the actors Linda Bassett and Mark Lambert – who played the condemned convict Liz Morden and the hangman Ketch Freeman. Mark tried to measure Linda's height to prepare for her hanging and to assess her weight. During the improvisation Linda didn't speak. But that night, at one o'clock in the morning, Linda phoned Timberlake. 'Look, Timberlake,' she said, 'I have to tell you this. I was *going* to speak…' And of course, in that scene in *Our Country's Good*, Liz *does* speak.

Another aspect of the workshop process that Timberlake found useful was to be able to bear our particular group of actors in mind as she wrote, moulding the characters of the various parts to fit the actors' own personalities, and occasionally changing some of the characters from *The Playmaker*. The hangman in Keneally's novel, for example, was originally a Cockney, but since Mark Lambert was Irish, Timberlake made him Irish in her play.

THE REHEARSAL PERIOD

Timberlake was given a total of two months to write the play, which she found a considerable struggle, working flat out from six in the morning until midnight every day. However, since there was no absolute demand for a finished play (see p. 11), she also felt a degree of freedom. 'My mind was somewhere else,' she says today, 'it was fantastically liberating. That was the good thing: no pressure.'

The basic structure of *Our Country's Good* had been predetermined by that of *The Playmaker*, so there was already a clear arc in place, and Timberlake had also added the story

WRITING 'OUR COUNTRY'S GOOD'

of Liz Morden and her decision to speak in two crucial scenes. But there were also long monologues in the opening scene, the backstories of all the convicts. These would be reduced to a few lines in the end. 'I knew in the first draft that I had something,' Timberlake says now, 'because it's something in your heart – you know you've touched something, but that's all I knew.'

Later on in the rehearsal period Timberlake, myself and some of the actors attended a performance of Howard Barker's *The Love of a Good Man* at H.M. Prison Wormwood Scrubs, given by long-term prisoners. Timberlake had by now already written a complete first draft but, as she recalls, that experience was 'a huge confirmation': 'It was one of those pivotal moments where you think, "No, I *was* right, because it is extraordinary to watch this performance by these prisoners. It has done something; it has given them a sense of self."'

During a typical working day at this time, we would rehearse a scene in the morning, while Timberlake was at home rewriting. Then in the afternoon we would present to her what we had worked on, and she would give us another scene. The play gradually came together, but Timberlake continued to make changes right up to the end. Act One, Scene Ten, for example, in which Mary Brenham and John Wisehammer discuss the meaning of words, was added after the first run-through (and only took a morning to write).

Timberlake was also inspired to quarry moments from the rehearsal room as material for her play. A good example of this is when she spotted Lesley Sharp, who would play the romantic lead Mary Brenham, crossing the room with a cup of tea and simply exclaiming, 'I love this!' This became Mary's last line in the final scene of *Our Country's Good*, completing her journey from a brutalised young convict to Australia's first leading lady. At the same time, the demanding stress of rehearsing two plays simultaneously also made its way into *Our Country's Good*. The actor Ron Cook was very reluctant to double the roles of Bullock and Brazen in my production of *The Recruiting Officer*, which the character Wisehammer – played by Ron Cook – complains about in Act Two, Scene Seven of *Our Country's Good* ('It'll confuse the audience…').

As in *The Playmaker*, a number of separate stories would provide the narrative structure of *Our Country's Good*: the romance between Ralph Clark and Mary Brenham; Harry Brewer's relationship with the child prostitute Duckling; and Harry's decline and death. But the story that interested Timberlake most, and which holds the play together, is the story of the amateur convict production of *The Recruiting Officer*. We see Ralph first casting the play, then arguing for its survival in the Officers' Mess (Act One, Scenes Five and Six), and we see various stages of its rehearsal. The final scene shows the convicts backstage preparing for their first performance, and at the very end we witness the first few moments of *The Recruiting Officer* itself.

None of us knew that *Our Country's Good* would prove to be such a great play. But by the end of its run at the Royal Court it was playing to packed houses, which was a clear indication. It resonated with London's theatre community, which then felt keenly under threat in Thatcher's Britain. And, of course, for Timberlake, it was a very personal triumph: 'The redeeming power of the theatre was autobiographical. The play is autobiographical, in a very indirect way, because it saved me; I mean, it did really save me.'

Ron Cook (as John Wisehammer) trying his luck with Lesley Sharp (as Mary Brenham) in Act One, Scene Ten: 'John Wisehammer and Mary Brenham Exchange Words'.

Synopsis

Act One

Scene One: The Voyage Out

A convict ship bound for Australia, 1787. The convicts huddle together in the hold while Robert Sideway is being flogged on deck. Ralph Clark counts the lashes. John Wisehammer reflects on the terrifying nights aboard ship and his desperate search for female companionship; John Arscott laments his hunger; and Mary Brenham questions how she got there.

Scene Two: A Lone Aboriginal Australian Describes the Arrival of the First Convict Fleet in Botany Bay on January 20, 1788

The Aborigine sees the First Fleet coming into Sydney Harbour and assumes it is a dream.

Scene Three: Punishment

Governor Arthur Phillip, Advocate General David Collins, Captain Watkin Tench and Midshipman Harry Brewer are shooting exotic birds at Sydney Cove. They discuss punishment in the new Australian colony. Tench and Collins want to build a gallows in order to hang three people recently found guilty of stealing from the colony's stores. Governor Phillip is against hanging, arguing that the convicts are criminals because they have never been offered anything better. Eventually he capitulates to Tench and Collins' demands, and asks Harry Brewer to organise the gallows and appoint a hangman.

Scene Four: The Loneliness of Men

Ralph Clark sits alone in his tent, writing in his journal. He addresses it to his wife in England, Betsey Alicia. Harry Brewer enters and confides to Ralph his guilt-ridden dreams over hanging the convict Handy Baker, and his own criminal past, as well as his insecurities about his relationship with the convict Duckling, now his mistress, and how he rescued her from hanging. He also reveals that Governor Phillip wants to put on a play. Ralph, keen for promotion and a fan of the theatre, asks if he could put in a good word for him with Phillip.

Scene Five: An Audition

Ralph Clark is holding auditions for the chosen play: Farquhar's *The Recruiting Officer*. Meg Long comes to audition. Thinking that Ralph is looking for women for reasons other than casting the play, she expresses surprise – all the convicts had assumed he was gay. Ralph dismisses her. Robert Sideway then enters with a theatrical flourish to tell Ralph how much he used to love the theatre at Drury Lane in London, and begs to be cast in the play. Dabby Bryant now enters with the shy Mary Brenham. As soon as he hears she can read and write, Ralph wants to audition Mary for the part of Silvia, the female lead in *The Recruiting Officer*, but the illiterate Dabby also wants a part in the play. Ralph says only that he will consider her for the part of Rose, a country girl, but she assumes the part is hers. Liz Morden enters at the end of the scene. Ralph wants her to read for the part of Melinda (a wealthy 'lady of fortune') but she grabs the script from him and says she will let *him* know.

Scene Six: The Authorities Discuss the Merits of the Theatre

The officers are drinking together late at night, discussing the prospects for the play, now scheduled for performance on the King's birthday. Major Ross is vehemently opposed to it;

Lieutenant Dawes, the astronomer appointed by Greenwich Observatory, would prefer to watch the partial lunar eclipse that night; the Reverend Johnson is concerned it will propagate loose morals; Captain Watkin Tench thinks the whole enterprise is pointless since criminals cannot be reformed. Governor Phillip argues that the theatre is a civilised pursuit: it may reform some of the convicts involved, and will anyway bring the officers and convicts together for an evening. Ralph claims that even in a few short hours he has 'seen something change' in the behaviour of the convicts, gaining confidence just from auditioning for the play. After some further debate, Collins calls a vote: the play is to go ahead. Ross is furious – 'theatre leads to threatening theory' – and vows to challenge the decision.

Scene Seven: Harry and Duckling Go Rowing

Harry takes a sullen and unresponsive Duckling out on a rowing boat. Fed up with his constant jealousy, she angrily accuses Harry of watching her all the time and keeping her from her friends. Harry seeks to placate her by suggesting she appear in Ralph's production, to which she agrees (though Harry promises to watch rehearsals in case she strays).

Scene Eight: The Women Learn Their Lines

Mary interrupts Dabby's solitary reminiscences of her home in Devon, encouraging her instead to learn her lines. Dabby responds by telling Mary she should make a move on Ralph since he is so obviously interested in her. But Mary feels guilty and ashamed of her past, and particularly aggrieved that Dabby 'sold' her to a sailor on the ship to get more food. Dabby dismisses her scruples – she knows Mary sports an intimate tattoo of a former lover's initials; proof she isn't a virgin. The women agree to differ, and begin rehearsing their lines – until interrupted by Liz Morden, who demands they help her practise her own scenes. It soon becomes clear that Liz can't read, and when Dabby mocks her about it, the two women fight. When Ketch Freeman arrives to break up the fight, all the women verbally abuse him for being the hangman.

Scene Nine: Ralph Clark Tries to Kiss His Dear Wife's Picture

Ralph is deeply troubled, pacing his tent and talking to his absent wife Betsey Alicia. He reads from the Bible. At midnight he kneels on the floor and kisses her picture, as he does every week. The hangman Ketch now enters unexpectedly, startling Ralph. Fearful of God's judgement on him, and ostracised by the women convicts, he eventually reveals that he wants to be in the play.

Scene Ten: John Wisehammer and Mary Brenham Exchange Words

Mary is copying out the script of *The Recruiting Officer*. Wisehammer is interested in what she's doing and they flirt gently, discussing the meaning of words from the play that relate to their own situation. Mary suggests he ask to be in the play.

Scene Eleven: The First Rehearsal

Ralph is leading the convicts in the first rehearsal, but Kable and Arscott, who have been cast as two of the main characters, haven't turned up. Liz Morden and Dabby seem to know why but do not share their information with the group. Ketch's presence is loudly resented by the women. Ralph rehearses Robert Sideway, who performs in a melodramatic manner. Black Caesar enters and insists on playing Sideway's servant, even though this is not in the script. Ralph gives up on Sideway and turns instead to Liz, trying to encourage her to act like a lady. Ralph introduces Mary Brenham into the scene. Duckling is reluctant to join in, refusing to play Liz Morden's maid. They are interrupted by Major Ross and Captain Campbell, furious that Kable and Arscott have escaped because of the rehearsal. They take Caesar, Wisehammer and Liz into custody for helping the escapees by stealing food for them from the stores. The rehearsal is left in chaos.

Act Two

Scene One: Visiting Hours

Liz, Wisehammer, Arscott and Caesar are chained in prison. Liz tells the others her story. Wisehammer declares his innocence. Arscott explains that he bought what he thought was a compass – in fact a piece of paper with 'North' written on it – from a sailor, and tried to escape to China. Sideway, Mary and Duckling come to visit them to continue rehearsing the play.

Scene Two: His Excellency Exhorts Ralph

Governor Phillip has heard that Ralph wants to cancel the play, since half the cast are in prison. Governor Phillip urges him to continue as he believes the convicts can be redeemed by the experience. He is particularly interested in the example of Liz Morden, 'the most difficult woman in the colony': 'How do we know what humanity lies hidden under the rags and filth of a mangled life?' He also convinces Ralph that it is vital to their own careers that the play does not fail. Ralph feels inspired and motivated to continue.

Scene Three: Harry Brewer Sees the Dead

Drunk and raving in his tent, Harry Brewer is haunted into madness by the ghosts of Handy Baker and Thomas Barrett. He screams for Duckling, who enters and tries unsuccessfully to calm him down. He is clearly very ill.

Scene Four: The Aborigine Muses on the Nature of Dreams

The Aborigine laments that the 'disturbed dream' of the First Fleet has remained in Sydney.

Scene Five: The Second Rehearsal

Ralph, Mary and Sideway are waiting for the rehearsal to begin. Major Ross and Captain Campbell bring in the prisoners, Caesar, Liz Morden and Wisehammer. Ross refuses Ralph's request to unchain Liz, and demands to watch the rehearsal. Ralph's claim that 'there is a modesty attached to the process of creation which must be respected' incenses Ross, who proceeds to humiliate the convicts. He makes Sideway display his back, scarred from the flogging on the ship, and orders Dabby to go down on all fours, and wag her tail and bark like a dog. He then wants Mary to reveal her tattoo – at which point Sideway starts acting, choosing words from *The Recruiting Officer* appropriate to the current situation: 'I shall meet with less cruelty among the most barbarous nations than I have found at home.' Ross orders Campbell to flog Arscott. Liz is too upset by Arscott's offstage screams to continue. In the same scene, Melinda says, 'Oh Mr Worthy, what you owe me is not to be paid under a seven years' servitude.' Most convicts were transported for seven years.

Scene Six: The Science of Hanging

As the delirious Harry Brewer looks on, Ketch tries reluctantly to measure Liz for her hanging, forcing her to stand up. He tells her he doesn't want to hang her, but promises to make it quick. Liz asks Harry to tell Ralph that she is innocent of stealing the food. Harry's hallucinations worsen and he collapses.

Scene Seven: The Meaning of Plays

The Aborigine believes the convicts are ghosts, wondering how they may be appeased, and made to disappear. Meanwhile, Mary and Ralph are rehearsing a scene as Dabby, Wisehammer and Arscott watch. Mary questions why her character Silvia asks Plume (played by Wisehammer) to make a will. This prompts a debate between Ralph, Wisehammer and Dabby which has more to do with Ralph and Wisehammer's affections for Mary than the play itself. Wisehammer asks Ralph if they can use a new prologue he has written. When the rehearsal resumes, Wisehammer kisses Mary, claiming it is right for his character, which riles Ralph, who decides to do another scene instead. Dabby becomes difficult, saying it is a 'silly play', too far removed from her life to be of interest. Sideway hasn't come to rehearsals as he is too upset about Liz, so Ralph rehearses Arscott's scene instead, but Dabby keeps breaking off. Then Ketch turns up, so Ralph begins to rehearse another scene, between him and Mary – but Mary refuses to act with the man who will hang her friend Liz, and the shambolic rehearsal is abandoned.

Scene Eight: Duckling Makes Vows

As Harry lies on his deathbed, Duckling implores him to live, promising to love him, but Harry dies.

Scene Nine: A Love Scene

Mary is rehearsing her lines at night on the beach in Sydney Cove, where she is joined by Ralph. The couple rehearse the love scene between Silvia and Plume, which doubles to reflect their own feelings for one another. They kiss, and begin to undress. Ralph says he has 'never looked at the body of a woman before'.

Scene Ten: The Question of Liz

Ralph, Major Ross, Governor Phillip, Captain Collins (the Advocate General) and Captain Campbell discuss Liz Morden's trial, trying to understand her silence throughout it. Ross claims it proves her guilt, but Ralph says it indicates 'the convict code of honour'. Collins is concerned for legitimacy of his court if the convicts don't trust it, and Governor Phillip distrusts the verdict. Campbell brings Liz in, but she still refuses to speak, until Governor Phillip says she must do so – for the good of the play. She didn't steal the food, she now tells him, and there was no use speaking before as she wouldn't be listened to. Governor Phillip orders a retrial, and tells Liz he meanwhile looks forward to her performance, to which she responds poignantly, 'Your Excellency, I will endeavour to speak Mr Farquhar's lines with the elegance and clarity their own worth commands.'

Scene Eleven: Backstage

Night. The Aborigine is dying of smallpox: the First Fleet is no dream. The actor-convicts are preparing to go on stage. Dabby prophesies the triumph of the play – and her own escape in the commotion afterwards. Mary tries to stop her as it will reflect badly on Ralph, but Dabby says she will refuse to go on if she tells him of her plan. Sideway rehearses his bow, and reveals his own plans to set up Australia's first theatre company, and Wisehammer promises to write him a comedy about unrequited love. While a search is made for the absent Caesar, Ralph offers his condolences about Harry to Duckling, and promises Mary that if they have children, he will name their son Harry and their daughter Betsey Alicia. Arscott arrives with Caesar, who has been drinking because of his stagefright: he is cajoled into continuing. Wisehammer recites his new prologue aloud, which comments on transportation –

> True patriots all; for be it understood,
> We left our country for our country's good.

Ralph says it is very good but too political to be performed tonight. He gives the actors a pep talk, and then the first performance of *The Recruiting Officer* in Australia begins to the sound of Beethoven's *Fifth Symphony*.

'The Recruiting Officer'

The Recruiting Officer was first performed in 1706 at the Theatre Royal, Drury Lane. It was written by George Farquhar – a young Irish playwright, born in Derry. Farquhar discovered his love of the theatre at Trinity College, Dublin, where he worked doing menial jobs in return for tuition. He moved to London and built his reputation with such comedies as *Love and a Bottle*, *The Constant Couple* and *Sir Harry Wildair*, all performed at Drury Lane. He joined the army in 1704, holding the post of recruiting officer, an experience that provided the raw material for the eponymous play. His later works *The Recruiting Officer* and *The Beaux' Stratagem* (allegedly based on his unhappy marriage, and written in six weeks from his sickbed) are still performed today. He died destitute in 1707 of tuberculosis, at the age of thirty.[1]

The Recruiting Officer can be described as a development of the 'Restoration' comedy – a style of witty and satirical sex comedy associated with the period following Charles II's return to the throne in 1660. It is a play in five acts and tells a tale of mistaken identity, thwarted love and devious soldiers. But Farquhar developed the form and brought a new level of realism to 'Restoration Plays'.

SYNOPSIS

Act One

It is early autumn[2], the weather is fine. The recruiting officers Sergeant Kite and Captain Plume go to the marketplace in the country town of Shrewsbury in Shropshire with grand speeches and money for bribes, to recruit the locals to the army.

Melinda and Silvia discuss their suitors – Mr Worthy and Captain Plume respectively. Melinda is justifiably angry with Worthy: in the past he has sought to make her his mistress unaccompanied by an offer of marriage. Now that she has inherited a fortune and is independently wealthy she resolves to punish him. Silvia chastises her for leading Worthy on, and announces her determination to marry Captain Plume, her love interest from the previous year. She also wishes she had the same opportunities as men: 'I'm heartily tired of my sex.'[3] She boldly declares that fidelity (constancy) is not of paramount importance to her.

Act Two

Plume demonstrates his love for Silvia by showing her his will, in which she is appointed the sole legatee of his (minimal) estate. News comes of the death of Silvia's brother, leaving her sole heiress to her father Justice Balance's considerable fortune. Balance now rejects the penniless Captain Plume's courtship of his daughter, and banishes her to the country. He has been advised to do so in a malicious letter from Melinda that confirms his low opinion of Plume. Silvia is torn between her duty to her father and her genuine love for Plume.

Kite attempts to recruit the local men Appletree and Pearmain by getting them drunk. Plume pretends to castigate him for it, and then recruits the men for himself.

Act Three

Plume is furious that Silvia has left without informing him, and Worthy is equally upset that Melinda has accompanied her. Despite his promises to Silvia, Plume thinks nothing of flirting with Rose, the country maid, in revenge for Silvia's desertion.

Melinda is walking by the riverside with her maid Lucy when they meet the flashy Captain Brazen, another recruiting officer, who boasts of his military deeds and showers her with compliments. Pretending to be seduced by his charms, Melinda walks off with Brazen in a deliberate snub to

Worthy. Worthy complains to Plume, who pretends to challenge Brazen for Melinda's hand, forcing her to run to Worthy for protection. As Plume and Brazen bury the hatchet, Silvia appears, disguised in men's clothes as 'Jack Wilful', a gentleman seeking to join the army. They quarrel over which of them is to recruit 'him'. But when they begin a sword-fight to determine the issue, Sergeant Kite enlists Silvia/Jack himself, carrying 'him' offstage. Burying the hatchet again, Brazen confesses his intention to marry Melinda.

Act Four

Still disguised as 'Jack', Silvia encounters Rose and her brother Bullock, who has also been enlisted in Plume's company. Testing her disguise, 'Jack' boldly kisses Rose, who responds by claiming that she is promised to none other than Plume. When Plume himself enters, Silvia decides to test his intentions by pretending to challenge him for Rose's hand, threatening to enlist with Brazen unless Plume relinquishes her. Plume agrees, at the same time admitting that his flirtation with Rose went no further: 'I am not that rake that the world imagines.'

Meanwhile, while out walking, Melinda pours out her true feelings for Worthy to her maid Lucy. She has visited a fortune-teller who told her she will die unmarried, and complains that Worthy coldly rebuffed her when she ran to his protection (in Act Three). They then encounter Worthy himself, with whom Melinda bickers – and when Brazen enters and embraces her, Worthy thinks he has been beaten by his rival. Melinda storms off in anger at his pretended indifference. But Melinda really *does* love Worthy, as Plume now assures him – at the same time as revealing that the famous fortune-teller is none other than Sergeant Kite, using this deception to enlist further recruits from the local population.

Melinda and Lucy consult the 'fortune-teller', who with Worthy's connivance tells Melinda she will meet her future husband the next morning at ten – but unless she prevents him from travelling abroad he will never return. Then Brazen seeks a consultation, as to whether he should marry the wealthy lady whose love-letters he shows them. By comparing the handwriting, Plume discovers that Brazen's correspondent is Lucy. He also discovers that it was Melinda whose letter to Balance resulted in Silvia's banishment to the country; she didn't desert him after all.

Act Five

The next morning. Still posing as 'Jack', Silvia has shared a bed with Rose for the night – but only to sleep, as Rose vociferously complains. Then a constable arrives to arrest 'Jack' for immoral conduct: brought before her father, Justice Balance, 'he' is put in prison. When later brought to trial, 'Jack' is ordered to enlist in Plume's company.

Meanwhile, Worthy arrives at Melinda's home that morning at ten to announce his imminent departure on his travels. Bearing the fortune-teller's words in mind, Melinda admits her previous cruelty, and promises her hand to him if he stays. She also admits that she was wrong to send Balance the letter about Plume. Setting off for Balance's house to redress matters in person, she asks Worthy to meet her there with Plume.

Brazen has been bragging to Plume that he is due shortly at the riverside to marry his wealthy lady – who Plume wrongly assumes is Melinda, as he tells Worthy when he arrives to collect him. When a messenger arrives with word that Melinda has 'put off' her trip to Balance's house, Worthy assumes the worst and dashes off to prevent the marriage. Arriving at the river, he finds Brazen with a masked lady, and challenges him to a duel – which the 'lady' prevents by unmasking herself as Lucy: her hopes of marriage to Brazen are dashed; and she explains that her mistress, Melinda, postponed her journey to Balance's house because Silvia has mysteriously gone missing.

This of course is because Silvia is 'Jack', as her father Justice Balance has realised, now taking the opportunity to test Plume's true character. Plume honestly confesses that he is innocent of any wrongdoing with Rose; and when told that 'Jack' is the son of an old friend of Balance's, he offers to discharge 'him' to his care for free ('Not a penny, sir; I value an obligation to you much above a hundred pound'). Fully satisfied, Balance tells Silvia he has rumbled her disguise, but instead of punishing her gives his blessing to her marriage to Plume. Plume forgives Melinda for her malicious letter, telling her that the only reparation she can make is to marry his friend Worthy; transfers his own company of recruits to Brazen; asks that Silvia employ Rose as her maid; and vows 'to raise recruits the matrimonial way'.

'THE RECRUITING OFFICER'
AND 'OUR COUNTRY'S GOOD'

The Recruiting Officer is intertwined with the convicts' and officers' lives throughout *Our Country's Good*. An understanding of Farquhar's play and its themes can enrich one's understanding of Wertenbaker's text.

For one thing, it can be difficult for a modern audience or actor to comprehend the officers' objections to putting on a play in the first place. But when *The Recruiting Officer* was being performed in Restoration Britain, it gave a candid and controversial picture of sexual relations. Titillating subjects were being openly discussed for the first time on the stage. Reverend Johnson's comments in Act One, Scene Six ('The Authorities Discuss the Merits of the Theatre') need to be explored in this light: 'I hear many of these plays are about rakes and encourage loose morals in women.'[4] In *The Recruiting Officer*, the characters openly talk about 'lying with' each other, and there are distinct gay overtones to Sergeant Kite's character – at a time when homosexuality was still a capital crime. In this scene (Act Three, Scene Two), Kite is trying to enlist Silvia who is dressed as a man, Jack Wilful:

> KITE. Pray noble Captain, give me leave to salute you.
> *Offers to kiss her.*
> SILVIA. What, men kiss one another!
> KITE. We officers do, 'tis our way; we live together like man
> and wife, always either kissing or fighting.[5]

Actresses were permitted to perform for the first time in the seventeenth century, and they were commonly seen as no better than prostitutes; as Reverend Johnson exclaims, 'actresses are not famed for their morals'.[6] However, Nell Gwynne had made it to the King's bedchamber, and her fellow actress Lavinia Fenton, the first Polly Peachum later became the Duchess of Bolton. Ross is outraged because he senses the danger of the convict women gaining legitimacy and becoming objects of sexual desire – 'Filthy, thieving, lying whores and now we have to watch them flout their flitty wares on the stage!'[7]

A modern reader can find a great deal of information about eighteenth-century sex and sexual relationships in *The Recruiting Officer*. In Farquhar's lifetime, marriage was principally about money, and finding a good match in the opposite sex in terms of status and property; and the same rules, with only slight variation, applied in Sydney.

The convict women, for example, were routinely described as 'whores' by the officers (and indeed by subsequent commentators). Prostitution was not a crime in itself in the eighteenth century, and it was not punishable by transportation. And although many of the transported women may have 'gone on the town' to supplement their income from other sources, few were out-and-out prostitutes. *The Playmaker* makes the point that the possibilities of upward mobility for the convict women were considerable if they were content to become the concubines or partners of the officers. In *Our Country's Good*, Mary Brenham, through the process of playing Silvia in *The Recruiting Officer*, rises from the status of 'filthy' convict to love interest, in the eyes of Lieutenant Ralph Clark. Becoming his mistress afforded her privileges not assigned to the other convicts – such as living in a decent hut.

Farquhar's theme of devious recruiting officers would also have been familiar to the transported convicts. Between 1702 and 1709, the English army grew from 18,000 to 70,000. There were two forms of recruitment: voluntary enlistment and impressment, whereby unemployed men of working age were forced to sign up against their will.[8] The recruiting officers got paid for every man they recruited, so throughout the play Kite and Plume try all sorts of trickery to enlist the local men. In *The Playmaker*, Ralph decides to change all the references to 'soldiers' in *The Recruiting Officer* to 'Marines', and all references to 'France' to 'America', in order to update the recruiting practices of 1706 to the late 1780s – the period in which *Our Country's Good* is also set.[9]

Timberlake cleverly uses the text of *The Recruiting Officer* still further to reflect the situation of the convicts in the following scenes of *Our Country's Good*:

Act One, Scene Five: An Audition

Ralph asks Mary to read from *The Recruiting Officer* to audition for the part of Silvia. The line she reads from the play (Act Two, Scene Two) – 'Whilst there is life there is hope, Sir' – refers to Silvia's hopes for her mortally ill brother, but in *Our Country's Good*, Timberlake could equally be referring to the fact that the convicts may gain some hope through the process of making a play.

Act One, Scene Ten: John Wisehammer and Mary Brenham Exchange Words

Mary is transcribing Act Two, Scene Two of *The Recruiting Officer*, in which Justice Balance sends his daughter Silvia off to the country. Wisehammer comments on some of the words from the scene: 'friend', 'country', 'indulgent'. This develops into a discussion about words relevant to his own life and the convicts' situation – 'injustice', 'innocent'.

Act Two, Scene Five: The Second Rehearsal

This is the most poignant use of *The Recruiting Officer*. Major Ross gatecrashes a rehearsal and torments the convicts. Sideway starts acting, playing the part of Worthy, Melinda's spurned lover: 'What pleasures I may receive abroad are indeed uncertain; but this I am sure of, I shall meet with less cruelty among the most barbarous nations than I have found at home.'[10] In *The Recruiting Officer* (Act Five, Scene Three), Worthy is commenting on Melinda's cruelty towards him, claiming war would be more tolerable. But in *Our Country's Good*, Sideway is commenting on Ross's barbarous treatment of him and his fellow convict actors.

Act Two, Scene Seven: The Meaning of Plays

This is a long scene in which *The Recruiting Officer* is used several times, and with various meanings. Ralph opens the scene as Captain Plume declaring his love for Silvia, played by Mary Brenham: 'For I swear, Madam, by the honour of my profession, that whatever dangers I went upon, it was with the hope of making myself more worthy of your esteem.'[11] This has a double meaning as it is apparent that Ralph is developing feelings for Mary. The rehearsal descends into a debate between Ralph, Wisehammer (both rivals for Mary's affections) and Dabby, which Ralph cuts short in order to rehearse Silvia's entrance as Jack Wilful instead (Act Three, Scene Two), and to block Wisehammer's ardour.

Mary (as Jack/Silvia) enters and Wisehammer (as Captain Brazen) kisses her. Ralph is outraged. Wisehammer justifies his kiss by saying that the eccentric character of Brazen would do such a thing – though in fact Wisehammer simply wants to reassert his designs on Mary, and to undermine Ralph.

Ralph now decides to move on again, and asks Arscott to do his speech as Kite: 'Sir, I was born a gypsy, and bred among that crew till I was ten years old, there I learned canting and lying.'[12] Dabby interjects by claiming that this is *her* life story! The convicts debate whether a play should tell people what they know or else something new; whether it should be set in the past or address contemporary issues.

Ralph moves on, once again, to another scene, this time featuring Silvia and Justice Balance, played by Ketch (Act Two, Scene Two). Mary begins, 'Whilst there is life there is hope, Sir' – but since her friend Liz is about to be hanged, she now feels that there is no longer any life or any hope, in direct contrast to the first auditions for the play. Mary cannot continue the scene.

Act Two, Scene Nine: A Love Scene

Mary is practising her lines as Silvia on the beach at night. Ralph enters, and recites Plume's line in reply: 'There's something in this fellow that charms me.' Mary then continues the scene: 'One favour I must beg – this affair will make some noise…' and the couple kiss.[13] Of course, for Ralph to even consider taking Mary as a convict wife will not only 'make some noise' by causing ructions among the officers; it also represents a sea-change in Ralph's thinking, since he has hitherto been obsessed with his wife in England, Betsey-Alicia. 'Will you lodge at my quarters in the meantime?' asks Ralph-as-Plume now: 'You shall have part of my bed.' In *The Recruiting Officer* (Act Four, Scene One), Jack/Silvia and Plume are actually quarrelling over the country girl Rose in this scene, but Timberlake has brilliantly used the lines to reflect Ralph and Mary's burgeoning romance.

David Haig (as Ralph Clark) anxiously supervises his first rehearsal. I know how he feels. (From left to right: Mark Lambert, Jude Akuwudike, David Haig and Alphonsia Emmanuel in Act One, Scene Eleven: 'The First Rehearsal'.)

Characters

THE OFFICERS

GOVERNOR ARTHUR PHILLIP (1738–1814) was a remarkable eighteenth-century man who rightly occupies a legendary role as the founding father of the Australian nation. His name is commemorated in streets, towns, islands and mountains all over the Australian continent. After a solid, but not brilliant naval career, Phillip had retired and was happily tending his farm in Hampshire when the Home Secretary, Lord Sydney, asked him to preside over the penal colony in New South Wales. He was picked for his superb organisational skills and unassuming nature; the government wanted competency, not a politician. Phillip held the post of Governor General from 1788 to 1792, when he returned to England.

Governor Phillip was a humane and liberal ruler: he wanted to live peacefully with the native Aboriginal peoples and insisted the convicts and officers had the same rations. In *The Playmaker*, Phillip features as a somewhat mysterious and solitary figure, a revered and perhaps feared ruler whose main storyline centres on his relationship with the Aborigine, Arabanoo (see p. 65). Known as 'His Excellency' (or 'H.E.'), his physical isolation prompts gossip among both officers and convicts as to his sexuality. This portrayal is perhaps more historically accurate than Timberlake's version of the character: the eighteenth-century class system would have rendered Phillip as unapproachable as a modern-day president or pop star. In terms of his sexuality, the historical Arthur Phillip was married for six years but divorced – and he *did* keep Arabanoo in a hut at the bottom of his garden in the same way as the officers kept their convict wives. Arabanoo's hut is now the site of the Sydney Opera House.

It was Phillip's intuitive humanity, allied to his belief in the potential for improvement in any human being, that Timberlake seized upon for her characterisation. Phillip is not just a historical character in *Our Country's Good*, but a representation of a liberal belief system that favours education and redemption over punishment. When writing the part of Governor Phillip, of course, Timberlake used the character from *The Playmaker*, together with the research gathered on the real historical figure. But she also drew on her own university days. 'I love Greek,' she says: 'I had a great teacher, who I partly used for Governor Phillip. He was an expert in the *Meno* [of Plato]. He was wonderful man, a German-Jewish refugee. But in the scene between Ralph and Governor Phillip (Act Two, Scene Two: 'His Excellency Exhorts Ralph') I also used some of Max's powers of persuasion.'

Phillip's humanist tendencies are repeatedly asserted in *Our Country's Good*. In Act One, Scene Three ('Punishment') he voices his objections to hanging and is instinctively repulsed by the idea of hanging a seventeen-year-old boy and an eighty-two-year-old woman. This is contrasted with the harsher, more cynical views of the other officers. He suggests it is possible to reform convicts through education and culture. When the other officers mock him, he retorts: 'We learned to love such things because they were offered to us when we were children or young men. Surely no one is born naturally cultured?'[14]

As Governor General he has the power of an absolute monarch over the Australian territories. It is interesting that he sometimes chooses not to use these powers, and instead opens himself to a process of debate and democratic decision. This is demonstrated in Act One, Scene Six ('The Authorities Discuss the Merits of the Theatre'), in which the officers debate whether to put on the play. Phillip could simply order the play to go ahead, but instead he allows the officers to vote on it. And in Act Two, Scene Ten ('The Question of Liz'), Phillip's powers would allow him to overrule the court and give Liz a pardon; instead, however, he defers to the process of justice and feels it necessary both to hear Liz's evidence and have it corroborated.

This insistence on democracy and justice is explained in Act Two, Scene Two ('His Excellency Exhorts Ralph'), where he declares:

> What is a statesman's responsibility? To ensure the rule of law. But the citizens must be taught to obey that law of their own will. I want to rule over responsible human beings, not tyrannise over a group of animals. I want there to be a contract between us, not a whip on my side, terror and hatred on theirs.[15]

Timberlake is presenting Phillip here as a progressive and learned man. In this passage he demonstrates his knowledge of 'Social Contract Theory', a burgeoning philosophical school of thought at the time, which argued that there should be a contract between the citizens and their ruler in order to better organise society in a more egalitarian manner. He also quotes the Swiss-born French philosopher Rousseau (1712–78), one of the most important writers in this tradition. Like his author, Phillip is widely versed in Greek philosophy. In this scene with Ralph he argues that the play must go ahead, based on the theory from one of Plato's great dialogues, the *Meno*:

> Socrates demonstrates that a slave boy can learn the principles of geometry as well as a gentleman... In other words, he shows that human beings have an intelligence which has nothing to do with the circumstances into which they are born... It is a matter of reminding the slave of what he knows, of his own intelligence. And by intelligence you may read goodness, talent, the innate qualities of human beings.[16]

Phillip hopes that by mounting a production of *The Recruiting Officer*, the convicts can prove this argument to be true. He is particularly interested in Liz Morden being involved, as she is notoriously 'the most difficult woman in the colony'. Her redemption through art will be an example to all.

MAJOR ROBBIE ROSS (*c*.1740–94) was the Senior Marine Officer in Sydney and, as such, de facto Chief Constable of the colony. In *Our Country's Good*, Ross is vehemently opposed to the idea of putting on a play. In Act One, Scene Six ('The Authorities Discuss the Merits of the Theatre'), he argues that 'the prisoners are here to be punished and we're here to make sure they get punished'.[17] This is a philosophy he pursues throughout, ritually humiliating the convicts in the two rehearsal scenes, and insisting that Liz Morden be hanged in Act Two, Scene Ten ('The Question of Liz').

The convicts fear Ross's sadistic violence, which he demonstrates in Act Two, Scene Five ('The Second Rehearsal': see p. 23). In return, he views the convicts as sub-human:

> I have seen the white of this animal's bones, his wretched blood and reeky convict urine have spilled on my boots and he's feeling modest?[18]

By today's standards Ross behaves appallingly and holds unattractive right-wing views concerning the rehabilitation of prisoners, but it would be a mistake to play him as an absurd tyrant.

Timberlake explains that his behaviour must be rooted in his character: 'You have to get into every character. I had to get into Robbie Ross and that was very hard, because he's a man and military – it wasn't exactly my thing. He was the most difficult character to make sympathetic because of the way he acted. But I did make a big effort to bring out his despair and hatred of where he was, and his self-hatred when he has that outburst about being in Australia – "I hate this possumy place".' What Ross wrote in real life was: 'In the whole world there is not a worse country.'[19]

Some of Ross's views are still given credence today. Billy Reid, an inmate at H.M. Blundeston was in a prisoner production of *Our Country's Good* in 1990. Timberlake went to see the production, and they remained in contact. He later wrote to her to describe how heartening and transforming the experience had been, and also of his disappointment that the prison authorities had dissolved the drama group soon after the production: 'It's a real pity the people who make the rules can't, or won't, see the sort of benefit a person can get from acting while doing a prison sentence... Obviously it didn't go down too well with someone with enough weight to block the drama group's progress. It's real sad when people like *that* are allowed to take such decisions.'[20]

CAPTAIN DAVID COLLINS (1754–1810) served as Advocate General of the nascent colony for eight years. Collins was a Marine officer with no previous experience of the law.[21] He returned to England after his initial eight years' service, and wrote 'one of the first and best books on the infant colony': his two-volume *Account of the English Colony in New South Wales*.[22] This established his reputation in England as an expert on Australia. Because of this status, the government asked him to become Lieutenant Governor of Van Diemen's Land (Tasmania) in 1803.

At the end of his life he formed a great bond and friendship with James Groves, a convicted forger. For a time, Collins even shared a house with Groves and his family. Collins died in Van Diemen's Land in 1810 and Groves was later buried near him. As Hughes writes, 'The friendship of these men was emblematic, suggesting at its most benevolent, and thus uncommon, level the interdependence between prisoners and masters.'[23] Perhaps Collins had absorbed some of these values from his observations of Arthur Phillip.

In *The Playmaker*, Lieutenant Ralph Clark looks up to and admires Davy Collins:

> Ralph... was unrancorously certain that Davy's book would be a journal of great quality and popular appeal, since Davy was a natural scholar. That did not mean he had ever been to Oxford or Cambridge – he had entered the Marines at the age of fourteen. But he had a scholar's nose – he was interested in everything to do with this strange reach of the universe.[24]

Collins appears in three scenes in *Our Country's Good* – Act One, Scenes Three and Six, and Act Two, Scene Ten. He is portrayed as a reasonable and intelligent man. In Act One, Scene Three ('Punishment'), he is firmer when it comes to punishment than Governor Phillip, advocating hanging – 'The quick execution of justice for the good of the colony.'[25] However, in Act One, Scene Six ('The Authorities Discuss the Merits of the Theatre'), he is happy to allow the play to go ahead. Collins's motivation throughout is the maintenance of justice in the colony. He is in favour of anything that supports the justice system and anything that doesn't affect it (the play), but wary of anything that may harm it (not implementing capital punishment). Perhaps this is due to his inexperience and determination to impress, or it could come from an innate sense of justice and fairness, similar to that of Governor Phillip.

This is demonstrated more fully in Act Two, Scene Ten ('The Question of Liz'). In this scene, Liz Morden has already been tried for stealing from the colony stores. She didn't speak and because she refused to give evidence was found guilty, even though the evidence against her was flimsy. Ross is determined that she be hanged, while Phillip is concerned that his liberal experiment will be proved a failure. However, for Collins the issue is justice:

> My only fear, Your Excellency, is that she may have refused to speak because she no longer believes in the process of justice. If that is so, the courts here will become travesties. I do not want that.[26]

CAPTAIN WATKIN TENCH (1758–1833) stayed in Sydney from 1788 to 1791. He wrote two books on Australia: *Narrative of the Expedition to Botany Bay* and *Complete Account of the Settlement at Port Jackson*.

While his convict ship was anchored in Britain, Tench had to censor the convicts' letters home. He wrote in his journal that the letters always referred to the dread of the voyage and fear of a barbarous land abroad; he was unsympathetic, dismissing these fears as 'doubtless an artifice to awaken compassion'.[27] Tench's journals also give us the first drawing of a 'kankaroo', and he records conversations with Aborigines. A street is named after him in Sydney.

After leaving Sydney in 1792, Tench was serving on the ship *HMS Alexander* off the coast of Brittany when he was captured by the French and put in a prisoner-of-war camp. It is rumoured that he escaped, stole a boat and sailed home, perhaps inspired by the story of Dabby Bryant (see pp. 58–60).[28] In fact, he too seems to have gained sympathy towards the convicts from his time in New South Wales. He wrote of Dabby Bryant's escape in his later journals:

> I confess that I never looked at these people without pity and astonishment. They had miscarried in a heroic struggle for liberty; after having combated every hardship and conquered every difficulty.[29]

Tench retired for the second time in 1827 and lived with his wife Anna Maria, the daughter of a naval surgeon, and their four adopted children.[30] He died in 1833.

Tench represents, in Wertenbaker's view, a philosophy of right-wing pragmatism, which was gaining ground at the time she was writing the play. In *Our Country's Good*, he demonstrates his youthful inability to empathise with the convicts. He says in Act One, Scene Three ('Punishment'): 'There is much excitement in the colony about the hangings. It's their theatre, Governor, you cannot change that.'[31] He also argues that 'the criminal tendency is innate',[32] in contrast to Governor Phillip's assertion of the convicts' innate humanity.

Tench reasserts these beliefs that society is unchanging and that the convicts are naturally criminals in Act One, Scene Six ('The Authorities Discuss the Merits of the Theatre'), where he adds a fuller explanation of his pragmatic reasoning:

> I would simply say that if you want to build a civilisation there are more important things than a play. If you want to teach the convicts something, teach them to farm, to build

houses, teach them a sense of respect for property, teach them thrift so they don't eat a week's rations in one night, but above all, teach them to work, not how to sit around laughing at a comedy.[33]

CAPTAIN JEMMY CAMPBELL (dates unknown) is Major Ross's inarticulate Scottish sidekick in *Our Country's Good*. In *The Playmaker*, Keneally imagines that Campbell was once a genial man, who enthralled the Officers' Mess with eloquent speeches, but 'Jemmy was Ross's main partisan, and the aloes in Robbie had now soured Jemmy too'.[34] As with Ross, it's important not to play Campbell as a caricature. He was a real person, and his dependence on Ross was partly about his desire for promotion, which Ross in fact recommended in a letter to the Admiralty. An inlet of Sydney Cove is named after him.

In *Our Country's Good*, Campbell struggles to make a fully formed sentence. According to Ian Redford, the actor who played Campbell in the 1998 production at the Young Vic Theatre, 'He's one of those people who gets all angry about things and can't quite finish their sentences. I played him as somebody who was keeping an eye on Ross all the time. Whatever Ross thought, he went with, he was on his side.' When rehearsing, Ian was asked to complete Campbell's sentences, in order that he fully understood what Campbell was trying to convey. He's also a character full of comic potential, especially in Act One, Scene Six ('The Authorities Discuss the Merits of the Theatre').

LIEUTENANT GEORGE JOHNSTON (1764–1823) took the Jewish Esther Abrahams for a convict wife. In *The Playmaker*, Keneally writes of his generosity towards the women convicts on the ship:

Lieutenant Johnston, who travelled on Penrhyn, had admitted and celebrated his love for Abrahams early on in the voyage, and one token of it had been this gift of bound magazines to the women's hold.[35]

His compassion for the women convicts explains his position in Act One, Scene Six ('The Authorities Discuss the Merits of the Theatre'): Reverend Johnson complains that Jesus didn't propose putting on plays for his disciples, to which he replies:

> He did propose treating sinners, especially women who have sinned, with compassion. Most of the convict women have committed small crimes, a tiny theft – [36]

Johnston had to return to England in the late 1790s for a court case. While he was away, Esther accumulated property, including a bakery with its own stores and an orchard. Johnston returned and married her, and she became one of the richest women in Australia.[37] He was involved in the 1808 Rum Rebellion, in which Governor Bligh was overthrown. He was tried back in England by court martial, but was allowed to return to Australia. A suburb in Sydney is named in his memory: Annandale, which was the name he gave to his property after his hometown in Scotland.

LIEUTENANT WILLIAM DAWES (1762–1836) is the central character of Kate Grenville's fine novel *The Lieutenant* (2009). As with the other officers, the twists and turns of the real events in his life are extraordinary. His isolated 'observatory', situated at Dawes Point just underneath what is now the Sydney end of the Sydney Harbour Bridge, gave him some independence from the other officers. His encounters with the Iora peoples provided him with the opportunity to make the first dictionary of Aboriginal languages, which is now lodged in the School of Oriental and African Studies (SOAS) library in London. He returned to England at the end of four years' service, and became an active campaigner for the Abolition of the Slave Trade. He died in Antigua, where he had been running schools for freed slaves.

Dawes plays a peripheral part in *Our Country's Good*, appearing only in Act One, Scene Six ('The Authorities Discuss the Merits of the Theatre'). In this scene he is not interested in the proposed play, since it will occur on the same night as a partial lunar eclipse. Dawes was fascinated by astronomy; in *The Playmaker*, the officers wonder if he is even part of their colony any more since he spends all of his time observing the stars or studying the customs of the Aboriginal peoples.

SECOND LIEUTENANT RALPH CLARK (1762–94) was a Second Lieutenant of Marines on board the *Friendship*. He kept a journal during his time in Sydney, which covers the years 1787–92. Ralph probably never intended to publish his journals; they were merely an attempt to deal with his desperate desire for promotion and his overwhelming guilt at leaving behind his beloved wife Betsey Alicia. As Hughes writes, 'He was not a writer but a miserably homesick young marine trying to set down his deepest emotional engagements in a language of sensibility derived from the genteel culture of the day.'[38]

Intriguingly, the volume covering the convict performances in June 1789 is missing and his role as 'director' of the play is probably fictitious. Despite this, both Keneally and Wertenbaker paint him as the keen champion of the play. Keneally writes of Ralph's quarrel with Ross about permitting the convicts to perform in the production: 'He knew at once that this was why people were theatrical managers – so that they could have this godlike excitement frequently.'[39] And in *Our Country's Good*, Ralph tells Governor Phillip he is ready to lay down his life for the play.

In *Our Country's Good*, Act One, Scene Nine ('Ralph Clark Tries to Kiss His Dear Wife's Picture'), Timberlake was drawing on a true ritual in Ralph's life. He kept a 'dear picture' of Betsey Alicia – a miniature under a hinged glass lid. According to Hughes:

> Each morning, Monday to Saturday, he kisses the glass. On Sundays he raises the tiny oval pane to kiss 'my dear Alicia's picture out of the case', the image symbolically laid bare, a little closer to flesh. This act is both a denuding and a prayer, as to the effigy of a female saint.[40]

Ralph's diaries recount his obsessive love for Betsey Alicia. She is held up as the perfect picture of feminine saintliness, in contrast to the convict women, towards whom he is scathing and abusive. The dreams of which Ralph speaks in *Our Country's Good* are also taken from his diaries. He records ominous dreams of violence and disturbance, including seeing dead lice on Betsey Alicia.[41]

Ralph was posted to Norfolk Island in 1790 – the dreaded outpost over a thousand miles from Botany Bay, which was to descend into a brutal, sadistic regime in the 1790s. He was accompanied by his now convict mistress, Mary Brenham. Ralph continued supervising the flogging of convict women to the end of his posting in 1791. However, at the end of his time on Norfolk Island he records stopping a flogging of fifty lashes after twelve strokes 'as she could take no more'. He records his surprise at this particular convict's offence, since he found her 'so fair of face'. Perhaps he had learned something from his relationship with Mary Brenham? His diaries also contain less frequent mention of his disdain for the women convicts as time goes on.

Ralph was reunited with his beloved Betsey Alicia when he returned to England in 1792; sadly, two years later she died in childbirth and the baby was stillborn.[42] Ralph's elder son died a few months later of yellow fever, as a nine-year-old midshipman on a boat in the Caribbean, and Ralph died in battle that same day.[43] But Ralph had one descendant – the daughter the convict Mary Brenham bore him.

Ralph is perhaps a more sympathetic character in *Our Country's Good* than his diaries would suggest. He goes on a remarkable journey during the play. In the opening scene, he calmly counts the lashes administered to the convict Sideway. In Act One, Scene Four ('The Loneliness of Men'), he writes to Betsey Alicia about the flogging of Liz Morden: 'The Corporal did not play with her, but laid it home which I was very glad to see.'[44] Ralph, like most of the other officers, is immune to the floggings as he sees the convicts as less than human. In this scene Ralph is dreaming of promotion

– 'If I'm not made First Lieutenant soon…' – when Harry Brewer enters his tent and mentions the possibility of a play. Ralph jumps at the idea: 'Harry, you could tell His Excellency how much I like the theatre.' But he remains dubious as to the idea of the convicts acting in the play. He talks of reading *The Tragedy of Lady Jane Grey* on the ship – 'But how could a whore play Lady Jane?'[45]

But after auditioning the convicts, Ralph's opinions already begin to change. He starts to see the benefits of the play, going to the extent of arguing vociferously for it in Act One, Scene Six ('The Authorities Discuss the Merits of the Theatre'):

> In my own small way, in just a few hours, I have seen something change. I asked some of the convict women to read me some lines, these women who behave often no better than animals. And it seemed to me, as one or two – I'm not saying all of them, not at all – but one or two, saying those well-balanced lines of Mr Farquhar, they seemed to acquire a dignity, they seemed – they seemed to lose some of their corruption… in a small way this could affect all the convicts and even ourselves, we could forget our worries about the supplies, the hangings and the floggings, and think of ourselves at the theatre, in London with our wives and children…[46]

Although his initial efforts are unsuccessful, Ralph takes to directing. In Act One, Scene Eleven ('The First Rehearsal'), he cuts lines, directs the actors to be more naturalistic, and takes charge of the rehearsal – at least until Ross and Campbell arrest some of his actors. This throws Ralph into doubt over the play, but Governor Phillip encourages him to carry on. In Act Two, Scene Two ('His Excellency Exhorts Ralph'), Phillip persuades him with philosophical arguments and the lure of promotion. Ralph is exhilarated by their meeting:

> PHILLIP. A play is a world in itself, a tiny colony we could almost say… And you are in charge of it. That is a great responsibility.
> RALPH. I will lay down my life if I have to, Sir.
> PHILLIP. I don't think it will come to that, Lieutenant. You need only do your best.

> RALPH. Yes, Sir, I will, Sir.
> PHILLIP. Excellent.
> RALPH. It's a wonderful play, Sir. I wasn't sure at first, as
>   you know, but now – [47]

This is a point of departure for Ralph. He is now fully committed to the play and his view towards the convict actors becomes much more sympathetic. He defends them against Ross and Campbell in Act Two, Scene Five ('The Second Rehearsal').

Once Ralph's commitment to the play has been established, his story becomes more focused on his relationship with Mary Brenham, which has slowly been building from the first audition scene. He is intensely jealous of John Wisehammer, his rival for Mary's affections. When Wisehammer kisses Mary in rehearsal, in Act Two, Scene Seven ('The Meaning of Plays'), he immediately asserts his authority over him: 'I'm the director, Wisehammer.'[48] But Ralph need not worry: in *The Playmaker*, it turns out that Wisehammer has been driving Mary up the wall by repeatedly going over his prologue with her.

In Act Two, Scene Nine ('A Love Scene'), Ralph and Mary get together. We haven't actually seen them together too many times in the play, but over the five months of rehearsal, this would have been a slow-burning romance that is finally coming to fruition. It is a monumental moment for Ralph Clark, who up until he met Mary Brenham thought that all convict women were 'whores' and the only woman worth looking at in the world was Betsey Alicia. 'Don't lower your head,' he says to Mary, 'Silvia wouldn't'[49] – showing how the process of Mary rehearsing the part of Silvia has changed her in his eyes; she has even become worthy of his love. Ralph's deep sexual repression also becomes evident: 'I've never looked at the body of a woman before.'[50]

In the final scene, Ralph's transformation is complete. He gives the actors assured notes; he is kind to the bereaved Duckling; he compliments Mary, and plans their future children (naming their daughter Betsey Alicia after his wife may seem to us the height of insensitivity, but it is probable that Ralph intended it as a compliment). Finally, Ralph gives the actors a rousing speech, incorporating what he has learned from both Governor Phillip and Mary:

> The theatre is like a small republic, it requires private sacrifices for the good of the whole... And now, my actors, I want to say what a pleasure it has been to work with you. You are on your own tonight and you must do your utmost to provide the large audience out there with a pleasurable, intelligible and memorable evening.[51]

SECOND LIEUTENANT WILLIAM FADDY (dates unknown) appears in only one scene of *Our Country's Good*: Act One, Scene Six ('The Authorities Discuss the Merits of the Theatre'). In this scene he is suspicious of Ralph's motives for wanting to put on the play. He assumes Ralph is angling for a promotion, which, of course, as they are of the same rank, is potentially damaging to his own chances of promotion.

Case Study

HARRY BREWER (1739?–96)

Harry Brewer was the first Provost Marshal in Sydney. He began his naval career aged thirty-nine after working for an architectural firm in London for fourteen years. He met Governor Phillip on the ship *Ariadne*, and they were to remain good friends. Harry Brewer dies of a stroke in *Our Country's Good*, but in reality he lived to relatively old age as Provost Marshal in Sydney. The year after *The Recruiting Officer* was performed, his convict partner, Duckling, was transferred to Norfolk Island; Harry didn't resist her transfer.[52] He is one of the most complex characters in *Our Country's Good*. His fascinating life story and detailed portrayal in *The Playmaker* can provide some illumination as to how to play him.

In *The Playmaker*, Thomas Keneally provides a rich and detailed commentary as to how he envisions Harry's life. In his youth Harry worked for the architects Cuxbridge and Breton in London. As the owners grew old, they increasingly relied on Harry, who was a good draughtsman, but they didn't realise he was embezzling large quantities of money to fund his habits of drinking and hiring prostitutes. One night Harry boasted to some women in a pub about his successful criminal activities. He found himself forced into a 'canting crew' (or gang) and had to swear allegiance to the Dimber Damber (the gang chief). Harry's guilt over his criminal past would haunt him in his later years.

Old Breton became ill and decided to check his affairs were in order. At this point Harry abandoned his position and joined the navy, aged thirty-nine. He was the navy's oldest midshipman, a junior post normally held by children and teenagers, beginning his career on the *Ariadne* with Captain Arthur Phillip. Mercifully, Phillip treated Harry as one of the adult crew and the two became friends.

Harry became obsessed with hanging even before he left for Australia. His conscience harried him, as he thought he deserved to be hanged as much as any of the convicts. Harry used to go to Newgate Prison the night before public executions, when it was possible to pay the jailer to sleep with the condemned women. In both *The Playmaker* and *Our Country's Good*, his obsessive guilt and fear of hanging fuels his alcoholism, which contributes to his hallucinations.

Harry's main relationship in *Our Country's Good* is with the convict, Duckling. *The Playmaker* describes Harry and Duckling's intense and strange relationship in detail, including the story of how Harry came to be so obsessed by her. A young jeweller's clerk in London had hired Duckling's sexual favours for an hour, and while he was asleep she stole a sack of candlesticks from him, and made off down Dean Street in Soho. But the clerk woke up, followed her and alerted the watch. Harry, who happened to be drinking in a pub on Dean Street at the time, witnessed the ensuing scene. When the clerk caught up with Duckling, her screams for help brought two young men from a nearby pub, who beat the clerk up before scarpering when the watch arrived. The jeweller's clerk handed her over to the watch, but out of embarrassment claimed he'd never seen her before, and that she and two men had mugged him on the street (a crime more likely to result in hanging than simple theft). Harry, with his fearful obsession with hanging, pleaded with the constables to let her go, but the clerk refused to change his story:

> Harry had attended her trial before the second Middlesex jury, who disbelieved the jeweller's clerk but still placed the value of the stolen goods at a hanging level. Harry had seen her accept the fatal sentence with a nightmarish composure. It was that – her terrible equability at the prospect of noose and lime pit – which had drawn him in.
>
> He had told Ralph the story of her reprieve every time they had drunk together, whether in Rio, the Atlantic, Capetown, the Indian Ocean, or at this new extreme of space. He was cruelly exercised by her strangeness, her incapacity to utter a tender word. He bore, by his own confession, the fear that she might one day say aloud that she might as well have been turned off, nubbed, in front of Newgate Arch – that a mouthful of lime meant about as much to her as a mouthful of air.
>
> He was also terrified that she might find a younger man. He did not want her to do it by Thespian success in the role of Lucy the servant.[53]

The actor Ian Redford played Harry Brewer in the 1998 production at the Young Vic. He sees Harry's relationship with Duckling as an extension of his alcoholism: 'There is an expression that alcoholics use, that they hold people "hostage". They say, "I'm all right, I've got a relationship, I'm okay," however bizarre or mad it looks to the outside world. He's controlling with her and he's a bully, but he desperately wants her to love him, to make him feel normal.'

Ian also played Arscott and Campbell in the production, and did a lot of research for his roles. He read *The Playmaker*, using a system of coloured pens – pink for Harry, green for

Arscott and red for Campbell – to make notes on it. He also made up a backstory for Harry – that he had been one of thirteen children, several of whom died from diphtheria, but that one of the local gentry had liked him and given him some education. Ian read other books, including *Phillip of Australia* (by M.B. Eldershaw, 1938), in which he discovered that Harry used to drink rum out of a little chipped cup, so he asked if he could have that in the production. He also read a history of hanging, in order to understand Harry's deep fear of it.

Harry Brewer's other key relationships are with Ralph and Phillip. Harry and Governor Phillip have a long history together, and as Ian says, 'For Governor Phillip, Harry Brewer represented a connection with the enlisted men, and for Harry it made him feel important.' Harry and Ralph are friends: for Harry, Ralph is a confidante; and for Ralph, Harry is a useful contact with Governor Phillip.

Harry has a monologue in Act Two, Scene Three ('Harry Brewer Sees the Dead'), in which he sees the ghosts of two people who have been hanged in Sydney – Thomas Barrett and Handy Baker, whom he suspects Duckling has cheated with. To play this scene, Ian and I began by talking about the drunks you see in the street talking to themselves. We actioned the scene (see p. 83–86) as if there were three characters present: Harry, Thomas and Handy. Ian gave each of the ghosts a voice – Thomas was a sly boy from Gloucester, and Handy a butch London Cockney. When we later rehearsed on the stage at the Young Vic I asked him to read it as a radio play. I sat in the darkened auditorium and gave Thomas and Handy's lines from different sides of the stage. 'Every night when I did it,' says Ian, 'I imagined Max was there, or the voices. Thomas Barrett was on the right and Handy Baker on the left, so I spoke to them both as if they were real people.'

Harry Brewer is a large and complex character, and this monologue can be tricky for actors. Ian dived into it in the first rehearsal, throwing himself on the floor: 'I felt the only way to approach it was to jump in and do it badly, then if it wasn't acceptable to bring it back.' One has to remember that the stakes for the convicts and officers were exceptionally high in this new and strange penal colony on the other side of the world, and this accentuates Harry's alcoholism and hallucinations. 'Play him as someone who's trying to be sane,' advises Ian. 'It's like trying to play drunk – you don't play drunk, you play somebody who's trying to be sober. Harry doesn't see himself as being mad at all. But the stakes are much higher than any normal fears or anxieties, so you can't play someone who is slightly drunk saying, "I'm quite scared about Handy Baker." He's terrified.'

*

THE CONVICTS

JOHN ARSCOTT was a carpenter. He was sentenced to seven years' transportation for stealing some tobacco and watches. In *Our Country's Good*, he is the brutalised 'enforcer' of the gang, who begins to take refuge in the play 'because I don't have to remember the things I've done'.[54] Arscott buys what he ignorantly thinks is a compass from a sailor, that turns out to be a piece of paper with 'North' written on it. Not far from Timberlake's mind was the extraordinary and horrid story of Alexander Pearce who, like Arscott, had escaped into the bush. Hunger forced him to turn cannibal and kill and eat his fellow escapees. In *The Playmaker*, Arscott becomes an enthusiast for the play, and he builds the set as well as the stage. Ian Redford, who played the role in the Young Vic production in 1998, says that Arscott 'becomes one of those converts, somebody who wants to run away – and suddenly the play becomes everything'.

BLACK CAESAR is determined to be in *The Recruiting Officer*. In *The Playmaker*, he is a thorn in the side of the officers, constantly invoking 'The Fragrant One' – his Madagascan God. He is feared by the convicts, and rapes Mary Brenham.

By the end of the book he is sentenced to be hanged. In *Our Country's Good*, by contrast, he insists on playing Sideway-as-Worthy's French servant, even though no such part exists in the script. He becomes involved in the camaraderie of the play, but endangers the production in the final scene by going missing before curtain-up, and getting drunk because of first-night nerves.

JAMES 'KETCH' FREEMAN was in real life transported for highway robbery. In *Our Country's Good*, however, he was a bystander in a brawl among some sailors and had the misfortune to be caught in the police round-up. He is forced into being the colony's hangman when he is accused of theft. Hanging was a spectator sport in England in the 1700s, and a whole language developed around it, including various names for a hangman – 'Jack Ketch', the 'crap merchant', the 'crapping cull', the 'switcher' and the 'roper'[55] – all of which are thrown at James in *Our Country's Good*. He wants to be in Ralph's play because the women convicts won't otherwise go near him. By the end of *Our Country's Good*, Ketch is as much as part of the acting company as anyone else, and seems to have taken upon himself stage-management responsibilities. The historical Ketch was eventually relieved of his duty, married and had seven children. He lived into his sixties.[56]

THOMAS SIDEWAY was convicted of stealing property valued at twenty-eight shillings in 1782 and was sentenced to be transported for seven years. He was sent on the *Mercury* to Nova Scotia, Canada, but escaped during a mutiny on board. In 1784 he was found 'at large still within the realm of Great Britain without any lawful cause', and was sentenced to death, later commuted to transportation.[57]

Sideway is a theatrical aficionado. In *The Playmaker*, Keneally paints him as almost obsessive. He confides to Ralph there that he would gladly steal anything 'which could give me genteel access to the best theatres. And those coffee houses where by spending threepence a day you can meet fine minds, Mr Clark, fine minds. And when it came to the theatre, Mr Clark, if I could not have a box, I was in a fever to sit by the spikes… The bars they put across the orchestra, to protect the actors from either hate or – and this was ever the case with me – adoration.'[58] Sideway was flogged on the ship *Friendship* for insulting Ralph and William Faddy. But in Australia, 'he was a different man; urbane, unlikely to descend to low insult for fear that might cast doubt on his capacity to act Mr Worthy the way Mr Munden would do it at Covent Garden'.[59]

In the final scene of *Our Country's Good*, Sideway vows to start a theatre company, and the real Sideway did in fact start Sydney's first professional theatre when he obtained his 'ticket of leave' and became an 'emancipist'.[60] The opportunities for acting in Sydney weren't great, but after Sideway's Theatre was started there were several further convict-theatre ventures. The theatre was successful enough for Sideway to buy a farm and land.[61] The theatre was on a site about 300 yards from Dawes's observatory (see p. 44).

JOHN WISEHAMMER stole a packet of snuff from an apothecary's counter in Gloucester and was sentenced to seven years' transportation.[62] In *Our Country's Good*, Wisehammer writes a new prologue for *The Recruiting Officer*. In fact, one of the convicts did write a prologue and epilogue for the play, but it is not known which. Watkin Tench recorded in his diary: 'A prologue and epilogue, written by one of the performers, was also spoken on that occasion which, though not worth inserting here, contained some tolerable allusions to the situations of the parties and the novelty of stage representation in New South Wales.'[63] The prologue we used was in fact written by a hack journalist back in London.

Wisehammer is also Ralph's rival in love for Mary. A serious, earnest, yet decent man, he laments in the final scene of *Our Country's Good* that he will write plays about unrequited love.

He also warns Mary in Act Two, Scene Seven ('The Meaning of Plays'): 'I would marry you, Mary, think about it, you would live with me, in a house. He'll have to put you in a hut at the bottom of his garden and call you his servant in public, that is, his whore. Don't do it, Mary.' Wisehammer is alluding to the fact that officers kept their convict wives in a hut at the bottom of their garden – by day they called them their house-keepers and by night they consorted with them as lovers.

Though Wisehammer never did get together with Mary, he eventually married a Cockney convict and became a respected merchant in Sydney at the end of his sentence.[64]

MARY BRENHAM had been a domestic servant and was con-victed of stealing clothes from her employer to the value of thirty-nine shillings. She was thirteen years old when con-victed, and eighteen when transported. Mary features in *The Playmaker*, where Keneally paints her as the daughter of ser-vants in a well-to-do household, thus explaining her higher level of education compared to the other convicts. When her father died she herself became a domestic servant. It was her mischievous boyfriend (the one for whom she gets the tattoo that Robbie tries to force her to show in *Our Country's Good*) who cajoled her into stealing the linen. Therefore, Ralph's assessment of her as a 'better breed of convict' derives from her background: 'This family history she had embarked on was, he was ecstatic to notice, proving her elegant, intelligent; a dazzling companion.'[65] Mary takes it in her stride that her relationship with the pedantic, propriety-obsessed Ralph will be limited:

> 'I will have you build a hut in my garden,' Ralph promised her. 'You shall be by name my housekeeper and by night my beloved.'
>
> She nodded. She knew that was the way love was managed on that particular penal moon.[66]

Mary Brenham became Lieutenant Ralph Clark's convict mistress and did indeed bear him a daughter named Alicia in

1791. Ralph left Australia three weeks after his daughter's birth. Conspicuously absent from Ralph Clark's diaries, Mary was eventually emancipated and became a free settler, but nothing is known of her later life.[67] Keneally tells us that she disappeared up country.

In *Our Country's Good*, she has been much affected by the voyage to Australia and is probably in a state of post-traumatic shock. In Act One, Scene One ('The Voyage Out'), she questions why she is on the ship: 'I don't know why I did it. Love, I suppose.'[68] This first line gives us an insight into Mary's romantic nature. In Act One, Scene Five ('An Audition'), it becomes clear that Mary doesn't have much control over her life – Dabby Bryant is trying to pimp her out to Ralph; she is shy and insecure; and she barely speaks, except to say the lines from *The Recruiting Officer* at Ralph's request, and even then she says them very quietly.

In Act One, Scene Eight ('The Women Learn Their Lines'), Mary speaks more freely, as she is alone with Dabby rather than in the presence of a male officer. She is already beginning to gain some confidence from the play, finding the strength to stand up to Dabby, something she has probably wanted to do for a long time: 'You sold me that first day so you and your husband could eat!'[69] She is keen to practise her lines from the play and is finding her niche as an actress: 'I have to be her [i.e. Silvia]… Because that's acting.'[70]

In Act One, Scene Ten ('John Wisehammer and Mary Brenham Exchange Words'), it becomes apparent that Wisehammer fancies her, and perhaps she to some extent reciprocates. In Act One, Scene Eleven ('The First Rehearsal'), she is really beginning to find her feet as an actress, and in Act Two, Scene One ('Visiting Hours'), her conversion to the theatre is complete: 'This is the theatre. We will believe you.'[71]

With Mary's theatrical passion and talents established, the emphasis in her story shifts to love. In Act Two, Scene Seven ('The Meaning of Plays'), she and Ralph exchange lines as

Captain Plume and Silvia in *The Recruiting Officer*. Plume is trying to reassure Silvia of his love for her, which is reflected in Ralph trying to express his love for Mary. Mary's romantic nature is reiterated; and when Dabby argues that women should always obtain a contract from their menfolk, Mary replies, 'Love is a contract.'[72] Wisehammer then takes her aside and tries to convince her to marry him, but in her next scene, Act Two, Scene Nine ('Love Scene'), Mary and Ralph finally express their feelings for one another.

In the final scene, Act Two, Scene Eleven ('Backstage'), Mary's relationship with Ralph is cemented, standing up for him when Dabby says she wants to escape after the play: 'The Lieutenant will be blamed, I won't let you.'[73] She and Ralph also discuss their future children. Mary's final line in *Our Country's Good*, 'I love this!', is an indication of the journey she takes – from a traumatised and shy convict, exploited by Dabby Bryant, to a confident leading lady.

MARY 'DABBY' BRYANT was a fisherman's daughter from Fowey in Cornwall. She was convicted of highway robbery and condemned to death, but her sentence was commuted to transportation. In *Our Country's Good*, Act Two, Scene Eleven ('Backstage'), Dabby prepares her escape from Sydney. She did, in historical fact, escape from Sydney in an open boat with her husband – the colony's resident fisherman Will Bryant – two small children, and seven other male companions. After an extraordinary voyage up the East Coast of Australia, they rounded Cape York, and rowed over the Sea of Timor to Jakarta. The Dutch Governor was moved by her (fictitious) story of a shipwreck, and put her on a boat for Cape Town. There she had the bad luck to be recognised by the detachment of marines from Sydney, who were on their way back to England at the end of their service. She was re-arrested, and Ralph Clark movingly records the death of her youngest son from fever on the voyage back. But her extraordinary story doesn't end there. Hailed in the press and in ballads on her return as 'The Girl from Botany Bay', she was granted a reprieve and lived to be an old woman in her beloved Cornwall. James Boswell – the Scottish friend and biographer of Dr Samuel Johnson – was in part responsible for obtaining this reprieve, sending her an annual pension of fifteen guineas (a guinea was a pound and a shilling). In thanks she sent him a sprig of 'tea', a native bush that grew round Sydney Cove and which she had taken with her on the voyage. It is now in the Boswell Archive at Yale University in America.

In *Our Country's Good*, Dabby is a pragmatic, mouthy and insightful woman. She is quick to try pimping Mary to Ralph Clark when she hears he wants some women for a play, and she muzzles her way into the play without giving Ralph a say in it. In Act One, Scene Eight ('The Women Learn Their Lines'), she declares: 'If God didn't want women to be whores he shouldn't have created men who pay for their bodies.'[74]

In Act One, Scene Five ('An Audition'), Dabby's first scene, she tells Ralph she can read dreams. In *The Playmaker*, Dabby recounts Ralph's nightmares to him, terrifying him by appearing to be able to read his mind. Dabby 'cures' Ralph of his nightmares in the novel – so it seems that he knew a woman, other than his wife Betsey Alicia, before meeting Mary Brenham.

Even in Act One of Timberlake's play, Dabby isn't that bothered about learning her lines for *The Recruiting Officer*, preferring to daydream about home. This is corroborated in Act Two, Scene One ('Visiting Hours'), when Mary, Sideway and Duckling go to visit the prisoners to rehearse the play, but Dabby doesn't bother to join them. In Act Two, Scene Seven ('The Meaning of Plays'), she repeatedly disrupts the rehearsal, arguing that the play is irrelevant and trying to change roles, rather than engaging in the rehearsal process. By the time of the final scene, Dabby expresses mild affection for the play, but reiterates that her mind is really on escaping back home:

I wasn't looking at the bow, I saw the whole play, and we all knew our lines, and Mary, you looked so beautiful, and after that, I saw Devon and they were shouting bravo, bravo Dabby, hurray, you've escaped...[75]

DUCKLING SMITH was a child prostitute who beguiled Harry Brewer (see pp. 50–51). Harry helped in commuting her sentence from hanging to transportation. In 1790, Duckling was sent to Norfolk Island due to the outbreak of famine in Sydney. Her subsequent fate is unknown.[76]

MEG LONG appears in one scene in *Our Country's Good*: Act One, Scene Five ('An Audition'). She is one of the lowest-status lags, filthy and stinking. Ralph is disgusted by her, and refuses to cast her in the play.

Case Study

LIZ MORDEN

Liz Morden is the only character in *Our Country's Good* that does not appear in *The Playmaker*, and is entirely fictitious. Her plot line is loosely based on the story of Nancy Turner, 'the perjurer' in Keneally's novel, who allegedly lies about her partner Dukes stealing food, but is let off due to lack of evidence. There are only two witnesses: a drunken officer; and Black Caesar, who is lamely looking to promote himself in the eyes of the authorities. Keneally implies that her reprieve may have come about because Ralph is so keen for her to play the part of Melinda in *The Recruiting Officer*.

Keneally's character of Nancy Turner is romanticised – she is beautiful and mysterious. Timberlake's Liz Morden is the antithesis of this. Liz's backstory came from research in the workshop (see pp. 11–14). Linda Bassett and Alphonsia Emmanuel interviewed a woman called Josie, who had done time in Holloway and Styal Prisons, and reported her story back to the company. It was extraordinary. Josie had started a life of petty crime as a child. The first time she broke into a house, she was staggered by the lifestyle of its inhabitants: 'I can't believe people live like this.' She stole a green jelly from the fridge. From there she got involved in more serious crimes, ending up in armed robbery.

There were two key things that Timberlake took from her story. Firstly, when Josie was twelve, she was brought before the Juvenile Court for crimes that her father had put her up to committing, after her mother had died. As Linda Bassett recalls, 'He stood up in court and said she was beyond his control. She was taken into care. She described that graphically – being taken out of court screaming at her father because she felt so completely betrayed by him.'

The second event in Josie's life that was particularly striking was an incident that occurred when she was in Holloway Prison. A gang of women had beaten up another inmate but had been found out, and thought she had grassed them up. She spent the night lying in bed, twisting a spring from the frame and sharpening it on the floor. In the morning she attacked the gang-leader with it in the washroom, thereby gaining respect among her peers. Josie was eventually helped by a teacher who came to Holloway and spent time with her. This gave Josie a sense of herself and allowed her to break her pattern of reoffending.

All the participants in our rehearsal were struck by how similar her story was to those of the convict women in *The Fatal Shore*. 'That just hit all of us,' remembers Timberlake, 'but it particularly hit me – and that was the character right there.' As for her first name, it presumably arose from the fact there were dozens of 'Lizzies' on board the First Fleet, a hugely popular name of the era for working-class women. Her second name, Morden, may carry with it associations with death.

There are two key scenes for Liz in *Our Country's Good*. Act Two, Scene One ('Visiting Hours') opens with a monologue recounting her life story. The language is difficult because it makes use of so-called 'canting' words – the dialect used by the working class in eighteenth-century London. Linda Bassett translates it as follows, but as she says, 'Most things mean *hanged*, *cunt*, or *theft* – lots of words for the same thing':

> Luck? Don't understand the word. Always leaves as soon as I turn up. I was born under an unlucky star. My father was a petty thief, didn't want to get hanged. Mum's left. Five brothers, I'm the only girl, so I take in washing. Then. My father. A woman's walking down the street, and he steals her handkerchief. She screams, he's arrested, says it's not me, it's Lizzie, look, she took it. So I'm stripped, beaten in the street, everyone watching. That night I take my dad's stick and try to kill him with it. I steal all his clothes and go to my older brother. He doesn't want me, I'm just another mouth to feed. 'Liz,' he says, 'why work for a living when you can sell yourself?' 'I'm not a pretty girl,' I say. 'I'm not asking you to be a good-looking girl, sister, men want your cunt, they're not looking at your face.' So I begin to sell my cunt. I think I'm in luck when I meet this posh man. He's dashing; and he has a different handkerchief for every day of the week. He says to me, 'It's not enough just to sell your cunt, Lizzie, it doesn't bring in the money any more, getting a bit older now.' He shows me how to rob the customers. So while a toff is shagging me up the wall, I see he's got a pocket-watch, and I steal it and run. But one time I ran too slowly, and the punter cries out for the police, the police hear, I'm arrested. 'Hanging' I think when I go in front of the judge, but no, the judge is a good guy, I get the King's pardon and it's transportation. Hunger on the ship, sailors won't touch me [i.e. she's completely diseased by now]: no sex, no food. But then when we arrive here, the Governor says, 'A new life, you could have a good time here, Lizzie, you could live it up.' 'Good bloke,' I think. It's not a bad play, and not too much work [i.e. she's obviously not taking the job from any desire for artistic glory!], and with a decent group of friends: Kable and Arscott – but no, Ross doesn't like my face; I'm arrested again, and now I'm going to be hanged. And that's Lizzie Morden's life.

It is important to research crime and poverty in eighteenth-century England to fully understand Liz's speech, but at the core of it is her deep sense of betrayal – a characteristic common to many criminals. At this point in the play, she was finally beginning to do something she enjoyed (rehearsing *The Recruiting Officer*) when Ross puts her in prison for allegedly stealing food. As Linda comments, 'Everyone in the story has let her down and now it's happened again, so she has got a sense of ill-usage and bad luck – "born under a ha'penny planet" is that awful doomy feeling people get: "Whatever I do I'm just doomed to have bad luck, but it's somehow everyone's fault but mine." '

Liz's mention of her 'good crew of rufflers' is worth exploring. As Linda explains, 'Arscott, who is only in [the play] briefly, and Kable, who you don't actually meet, become Lizzie's replacement family. The other women aren't really friends with her – she's the lowest of the low.'

Up to this point, Liz's lines have been short and gruff. Here, though, at the beginning of Act Two, she lets rip. 'She's been struggling with George Farquhar's language,' comments Linda, 'and for the first time this is her talking, so she can say it really easily.' But as Sally Rogers, who played Liz in the 1998 revival, points out, it's also important not to go over the top emotionally: 'You can be tempted – and indeed I was – to be a little bit reflective and maudlin, and you're damned if you do it like that. You have to attack it like a saxophone solo. I tried to weave little colours into it, which get lost when you're playing that level of rawness.'

At the end of the scene, some of the other convicts arrive to rehearse the play with her and the others. Linda argues that this is a key turning point for Liz: 'It literally saves her life when they come to rescue her,' she says. 'Even though she rejects them, the very fact that they've come is extraordinary to her.'

The second key scene for Liz is Act Two, Scene Ten ('The Question of Liz'). In this scene, Governor Phillip, the Advocate Davy Collins, Ralph Clark, Robbie Ross and Jemmy Campbell are discussing her recent trial in which she didn't speak. Ross wants her to be hanged. The key to the scene is that Phillip could simply reprieve her, so the question is, why doesn't he? He is determined that she defend herself to prove that 'the most difficult woman in the colony' has learned something through the process of the play.

Liz doesn't speak until towards the end of the scene named after her. As Linda says, 'When Davy says she must speak, "for the good of the colony", it wasn't going to cut any mustard at all; it's only Phillip mentioning the play, "Don't you want to be in it, Liz?"… The play was like being given something beautiful and something precious.' This of course proves Phillip's point about reform through education and, through this, Timberlake's thesis about the power of theatre to effect change in people's lives.

It is important to explore why Liz doesn't speak up to this point. Ralph argues it is because of the 'convict code of honour'. Linda enlightens us: 'She's been schooled in that since she was tiny by her gang of brothers, and replicates that in the colony with the crew of rufflers. So for her to betray them is huge, which is why she doesn't. She's going against everything she's ever lived by. If you think about her life, with no anchors in it and all that mistreatment, no one seeing any good in her, this code of honour, although the officers scorn it, is actually very important; it gives her a sense of integrity.'

This scene is the arrival point for Liz. When she says, 'Your Excellency, I will endeavour to speak Mr Farquhar's lines with the elegance and clarity their own worth commands,'[77] she has found an eloquence in a language that hasn't been hers up to that point; she has learned something from the play. Linda Bassett adds, 'To me, that last line was about finding self-respect and a sense of pride that didn't come from the club of rufflers where she had to obey odd arcane rules. She could hold her head up and look someone in the eye.' And for Sally Rogers, 'It felt like everyone liked each other in the play. It was a circumstance and a luxury she hadn't been afforded before.'

Liz Morden has one of the biggest journeys of all the characters in *Our Country's Good*. At the beginning of the play she is feared and loathed by the other convict women, and notorious for her behaviour among the officers. As Joe White[78], the assistant director in the 1998 revival, comments, 'If she gets into a fight she wouldn't be able to stop' – the very characteristic that that makes her so feared by the other convicts. 'The key to playing Liz is her status,' agrees Linda: 'She may be the lowest of the low but if you only play that, you don't get anything. Because she's living in a convict world, she's got a really high status because she's dangerous. And particularly when she's under sentence of hanging, that ups her status enormously; if you're going to be hanged, you're top. That's really important.'

However, by the end of the play, the other convict actors have visited her in prison, and have refused to rehearse with her hangman: they see her as a friend. Linda Bassett again: 'I know of course Mary's the leading lady, but so is Liz. Becoming Melinda gives structure to that. If you only play the bottom end, you don't get Liz; you've got to play the top end too, and the way the others treat her *as* a leading lady.'

*

OTHER CHARACTERS

THE ABORIGINE appears four times in *Our Country's Good*. In *The Playmaker* the Aborigine is called Arabanoo, and his story is fascinating. Ralph Clark and George Johnston are sent out to find two 'natives' to bring back to the convict camp. They manage to take one: Arabanoo. Governor Phillip builds a hut for him at the bottom of his garden, and gives him clothes and food, much to the consternation of Robbie Ross. Arabanoo calls Phillip 'Be-anna', the Gayamai tribe's word for 'Father'. The convicts are slightly bemused by this relationship and speculate as to its true nature: 'Everyone said that the native was captivated by H.E. – some said unkinder things still.'[79] The story culminates in Arabanoo's death from smallpox, which devastates the Governor.

Governor Phillip did indeed keep an Aboriginal friend in Sydney, but his name was Bennelong and he was an Iora tribesman, who travelled back to England with Phillip in 1792 and returned to Sydney in 1795 with the new Governor, John Hunter. Unfortunately, on his return Bennelong no longer fitted in with either his own tribesmen or the white settlers, who grew increasingly hostile to the Aborigines after Phillip's departure in 1792. Bennelong died in 1813, a forty-year-old alcoholic.[80] The Sydney Opera House is now located on Bennelong Point, the original site of his hut in 1789.

Timberlake was interested in including this storyline in *Our Country's Good*, but it would have made the play too long and complex. Instead, the Aborigine in her play represents ways of seeing; he is an innocent bystander witnessing the arrival of the First Fleet with bemusement and wonder. As Timberlake says, 'The play is about how you see things, how you see people – this is what he saw, this is how he saw the people.' Timberlake used a book by Keith Willey called *When the Sky Fell Down* (1979) to research the character, and the Aborigine's monologues are taken from precise descriptions recorded in this book. Since the settlers were white, for example, the Aborigines saw them as ghosts, and their full-rigged ships were thought to be giant canoes. The Aborigine struggles to comprehend the arrival of the First Fleet in the terms and language of the 'Dreamtime' – the stories of creation handed down through generations of Aboriginal culture.

REVEREND JOHNSON only appears in Act One, Scene Six ('The Authorities Discuss the Merits of the Theatre'), where he expresses his concerns over whether the play will propagate immoral thoughts and behaviour among the convicts. Reverend Johnson plays a larger part in *The Playmaker*, where his friend Ralph Clark remains wary of his evangelism:

Dick's sermons were dreadful – a mixture of plain moral advice as H.E. had requested, but also warnings to the lags about falling into the Papist heresy of Pelagianism and Justification by Works. When it came down to it, Dick considered that a whore or a pickpocket could always reform and be redeemed, but a heretic was beyond help.[81]

There is a hilarious chapter in *The Playmaker*, 'The Morality of Plays', in which Dick Johnson gets dreadfully worked up at the prospect of the play, and falls out with Ralph.

David Haig (as Ralph) stares meaningfully at Lesley Sharp (as Mary) in Act Two, Scene Nine: 'A Love Scene'.

Rehearsing the Play

HISTORICAL CONTEXT AND RESEARCH

'The past is a foreign country,' wrote L.P. Hartley; 'they do things differently there.' Any production set in the past has to discover the differences between now and then, and a lot of the exercises I did with the actors in the early weeks of rehearsing *Our Country's Good* focused on that. There are some simple questions to answer: What did they eat? How much did they drink? Impossible questions like: What did Mary Brenham think of calling her daughter after Ralph Clark's wife? Did she have any say in it? And obvious questions like: Why did people become criminals? What are the similarities? What has changed?

'Can we get on with the scene,' asks Arscott in Act Two, Scene Seven ('The Meaning of Plays'), 'and stop talking?' It's a common belief that doing things in rehearsal is fun but talking about them is less interesting. But it's not as simple as that: no exercise or improvisation can be detailed unless you have absorbed the information first. Read the first few chapters of *The Fatal Shore* by Robert Hughes. Remember that most of the characters in *Our Country's Good* were real people whose lives began before and ended after the play itself.

The events and characters of the play are framed by two real moments of history: the landing of the First Fleet at Botany Bay on 26 January 1788, and the performance by a group of convicts of George Farquhar's *The Recruiting Officer* in a convict hut on 4 June 1789 to celebrate the King's birthday.

Wertenbaker's play is essentially fictitious, but a study of that particular time span is essential to the student or actor to place the events of the play in context. It is important to look at both local events in the colony, such as the rationing of supplies and the threat of starvation, and international events, including the French Revolution, the commencement of Britain's long war against France, and the King's madness.

In this section we will look at crime and punishment in the eighteenth century, transportation, Australia, and eighteenth-century theatre.

Crime and Punishment in Eighteenth-Century Britain

The Georgian era of British history ran from 1714 to 1830, encompassing the reigns of George I, George II, George III and George IV. *Our Country's Good* is set in 1789, when George III sat on the throne. His reign was characterised by military conflicts in America and France but also by his mental illness, which is now thought to have been porphyria.

The Georgian era was a time of immense inequality, and life for the poor was extremely harsh. This was compounded by the huge increase in population. The population of England and Wales remained steady at about six million from 1700 to 1740; but from 1750 to 1770 the population of London doubled, swelling to a massive eighteen million by 1851.[82] The labour market was saturated with the young, causing mass unemployment. There was no formal police force, so enterprising youngsters turned to a life of crime.[83]

It was commonly thought that there was a 'criminal class'. This was not wholly inaccurate – in 1797 a staggering one person in eight lived off crime in London – but Georgian statistics were extremely inaccurate and many people were lumped into the 'criminal class' who were merely poor or 'immoral'.[84]

Punishments for crimes against property were severe, as property owners were terrified by the threat of the 'mob' or gangs. But as Hughes points out, the threat from the 'criminal class' was overhyped: 'It was a largely fantastical notion, exaggerated and nourished by deep-rooted territorial instincts. Gangs certainly existed in Georgian England, but they were only responsible for a fraction of the deeds that the law defined as criminal. Crime was still a cottage industry, a jumble of individual acts of desperation.'[85]

The political culture of the time was dominated by the theories of John Locke (1632–1704), who argued that people had a *right* to defend their property, an idea which permeated the American Constitution written in 1787, and would have contributed to the cult of property of the time.

Britain's European neighbours mocked its lack of police force and the lenient judicial system whereby defendants were afforded some rights, such as being innocent until proven guilty.[86] Because detection of crimes was woefully incompetent, and trials, while extraordinarily brief, were relatively fair, the Georgians needed another way to deter crime – and that was capital punishment: execution by hanging.

The Georgians concocted over two hundred hanging offences, from poaching a rabbit to appearing on a high road with a sooty face, and the vast majority of such offences were crimes against property.[87] Between 1749 and 1808, 1,776 people were publicly hanged in London.[88] Hangings drew massive crowds; it could be argued it was the theatre of the day.

However, from 1779 to 1788, when the convicts in *Our Country's Good* would have been sentenced, there were 1,152 capital convictions but only 531 executions.[89] Pardons were frequently dispensed and consequently Britain's prisons were overflowing. Georgian prisons were a world apart from their modern equivalent. There was no concept of reform; rather, criminals were thrown in together, whatever their age, sex or crime, in order to be locked up, out of sight of the general populace. Prison was a place to contain and control the 'criminal class'; a way to forget about it.

In Act One, Scene Two ('Punishment') of *Our Country's Good*, Governor Phillip discusses the prospect of punishment in the new Australian colony with Captain Watkin Tench and the Advocate General, David Collins. Tench and

Collins are keen to erect a gallows, resembling those at Tyburn in London, in order to hang three people who stole food from the colony's stores. Theft, as a crime against property was treated harshly in Britain, but the Australian colony was not self-supporting and starvation was a reality; in this context stealing food became a capital offence.

When Governor Phillip asks, 'Was it necessary to cross fifteen thousand miles of ocean to erect another Tyburn?',[90] he is demonstrating one of John Locke's other contributions to the political culture of the time: the argument that people can be changed by education. As Locke wrote, 'I think I may say that of all the men we meet with, nine parts of ten are what they are, good or evil, useful or not, by their education.'[91]

In response to Phillip's question, Collins argues that hanging serves as a deterrent: 'I suspect your edifice will collapse without the mortar of fear.'[92] Collins as the Advocate General in the new colony reflects the Georgian lawmakers' official stance on hanging, believing that such public punishment would reform its spectators. Georgian parents would take their children to watch a hanging and flog them afterwards, 'that they might remember the example they have seen'.[93] As Hughes comments, 'The scaffold was the altar of a ritual whose aim was to fill society with moral awe. This expiatory theatre, solemn and fatal, deserved the widest audience.'[94]

Tench takes a harsh and cynical view in the play, arguing that 'the criminal tendency is innate'.[95] He mocks Governor Phillip's attempts to argue for education, claiming there is no chance of redemption or change for the convicts. Tench represents the view of the general population in Georgian Britain.

This thinking (that criminality was innate to the 'criminal class' and that they should be contained out of sight), combined with severe prison overcrowding, led to the concept of transportation. A popular song in London starkly demonstrates the general unsympathetic disdain for criminals and support for their removal from the country:

Let us drink a good health to our schemers above,
Who at length have contrived from this land to remove
Thieves, robbers and villains, they'll send 'em away,
To become a new people at Botany Bay.
Some men say they have talents and trades to get bread,
Yet they sponge on mankind to be clothed and fed,
They'll spend all they get and turn night into day,
Now I'll have all such sots sent to Botany Bay.
There's whores, pimps and bastards, a large costly crew,
Maintained by the sweat of a labouring few,
They should have no commission, place, pension or pay,
Such locusts should all go to Botany Bay.[96]

Transportation

Official transportation began in 1717. Britain's unwanted criminals were sent to work in the American colonies and over the next sixty years, 40,000 men, women and children were transported there.[97] But the loss of the American War of Independence (1775–83) meant a new solution had to be found. By 1784 the prison crisis was getting out of control. Prisons, including the newly opened Newgate, were overflowing and the surplus was crowded onto ships, known as 'hulks', in British sea ports. The threat of epidemic terrified the locals, and the situation was unsustainable. The Prime Minister, William Pitt, came under enormous pressure to find a new penal colony.

Captain Cook 'discovered' Australia in 1770, including Norfolk Island, where he came across huge pine trees and flax plants – Georgian ship-building materials. Several locations were suggested for transporting convicts, including Western and Southern Africa, but the pines and flax of Botany Bay gave it the edge. In geopolitical terms it also gave Britain a stake in a new continent.[98]

Between 1787 and 1868, approximately 160,000 men and women were transported to Australia.[99] Transportation was a largely improvised operation, which is shown in the stark contrast between the so-called First and Second Fleets.

On the morning of Sunday 17 May 1787, eleven ships left Portsmouth Harbour with 16,000 miles and eight months of open sea ahead of them. In this First Fleet there were 1,500 people on board; 736 were convicts, of which forty-eight died on the voyage. In the light of subsequent fleets, this can be seen as a comparatively low mortality rate, which can be credited to Governor Phillip's planning and humanity. Furthermore, the First Fleet was organised by the navy, but transportation was subsequently contracted out to private companies, more interested in turning a profit than ensuring the convicts' safe passage to Australia.

This was the case with the horrendous Second Fleet of 1789–90. The contractors for the Second Fleet – Camden, Calvert and King – had been slave traders. The ships had been provisioned at a flat rate of £17.7s.,6d. per convict, 'whether they were landed alive or not'.[100] They therefore had no respect for the convicts and treated them in an unimaginably inhumane and brutal manner. As Hughes tells us, 'More than a thousand had embarked, but a quarter of them died at sea, and half were landed helplessly ill at Sydney Cove.'[101]

The contractors had equipped the Second Fleet with leg shackles[102] designed for African slaves on the dreadful 'Middle Passage' from Africa to America; the captain of *The Surprize* reported that 'it was impossible for them to move but at the risk of both their legs being broken'.[103] In the heavy seas of the Southern Ocean, water sluiced over the convicts. They lay there, 'chilled to the bone on soaked bedding, unexercised, crusted with salt, shit and vomit, festering with scurvy and boils',[104] and the ship was alive with rats, cockroaches, fleas and bugs and vermin of all sorts. The stink of the convict boats could offend other boats at two or three miles' distance if they were downwind.

Hughes quotes a letter from one convict, Thomas Milburn, back to his parents in England:

> When any of our comrades that were chained to us died, we
> kept it a secret as long as we could for the smell of the dead
> body, in order to get their allowance of provision, and many

a time have I been glad to eat the poultice that was put to my leg for perfect hunger. I was chained to Humphrey Davies who died when we were about halfway, and I lay beside his corpse about a week and got his allowance.[105]

There was a brief official flap about the shocking conditions of the Second Fleet but Camden, Calvert and King had already been granted the contract for the Third Fleet. The Third Fleet carried 1,864 convicts, and one man in ten died on the voyage. This was one-third of the death rate of the Second Fleet but still too much to countenance, and the company was not contracted again.[106]

The brutality of the Second and Third Fleets prompted an inquiry back in London. Gradually the Navy Board absorbed the lessons and improved conditions on the convict ships. Surgeon-Superintendents were appointed on each boat, who were answerable to the navy rather than the private contractors. Their job was to supervise the contractors' surgeons, prevent abuse of the convicts, supervise their health, and ensure the cleanliness of the boat, including the regular airing of bedding.[107]

While transportation improved, the journey was never easy. The ships were always cramped and desperately uncomfortable. The convict transports were not Royal Navy ships, and no ship was ever custom-built as a convict transport. Instead, they were merchant ships hired by the navy and adapted by naval carpenters at Greenwich. The carpenter's plan for adapting *The Atlas*, which made several convict transport voyages commencing in 1810, shows a double deck, with wooden bunks stretching the length of the hull. One privy is provided for 166 convicts. As Robert Hughes explains:

> the 'tween-deck plans of the First Fleet transports are lost, but the quarters were certainly very cramped for the marines and crew, let alone for the convicts: four transportees lying in a space seven feet by six feet, the dimensions of a modern king-size bed, were the norm. There was little headroom; Scarborough, the second-largest transport, had only four feet, five inches, so that even a small woman had to stoop and a full-grown man had to bend double.[108]

Despite the harsh conditions, transgression was never com-
monplace on the convict ships. There is only one instance of
a successful mutiny – aboard the *Lady Shore* in 1797 – and
this was instigated by the guard, not the transportees.[109] But
the constant fear of mutiny was very present for the captains;
the security guards were foreign mercenaries while the crews
contained a high proportion of press-ganged men[110] who
were intuitively in sympathy with the convicts, and who
shared the same diet and rough conditions.

The harsh punishment of flogging was a strong deterrent.
Our Country's Good begins with a flogging and Arscott is
flogged offstage in Act Two, Scene Five ('The Second
Rehearsal') for trying to escape the colony. Marcus Clarke's
1874 novel, *For the Term of His Natural Life*, includes an
account of his hero enduring a brutal flogging in which the
skin is stripped off his back; the flogger would have a run-up
as long as a fast bowler, and the novelist describes the groove
his feet made in the dirt at the point of delivery.

Many characters in *Our Country's Good* were given a 'condi-
tional pardon'. This meant that their death sentences were
commuted to transportation rather than imprisonment. In
Act One, Scene One ('The Voyage Out'), the convicts talk of
the extreme hardship on the boat. Wisehammer recounts the
general desperation to copulate, and this is reflected in
Johnny White's diaries, surgeon on board Dabby Bryant's
ship, the *Charlotte*, who records his amazement at the determination of the women convicts to break through the
bulkheads to gain access to members of the crew or the male
convicts.[111] Presumably it served to remind them that they
were at least human.

The voyage affected all the characters in *Our Country's
Good* in different ways. Liz Morden, the toughest of the
women, seems to have accepted it as simply part of her
horrid life story. She devotes merely one line to it in her
monologue: 'Jesus Christ the hunger on the ship, sailors
won't touch me: no rantum scantum, no food.'[112] On the

other hand, Timberlake has characterised Mary Brenham as an innocent country girl who at the beginning of the play is still in post-traumatic shock from the horrors of the voyage: Dabby Bryant pimped her to a sailor so she and her husband could get more food. Mary resents Dabby for this and feels deeply ashamed: 'I'll never wash the sin away.'[113]

In rehearsals I worked with the actors on imagining what life was like on board ship. I asked questions such as 'What qualities would help you survive?', 'Who would your best friend have been?', 'What romances endured under these circumstances?', 'Would Kable, Arscott and Liz Morden have risen to the top in this environment?'

We also played a game which I called 'The Transportation Game'. The actors got into small groups, each of which created a communal character and individual biography. Each of these collective characters legitimately earned £20 a year, but needed £40 to survive. The character was therefore likely to be forced to commit crimes to cover this shortfall.

I was the dealer, and dealt each group three playing cards. These cards indicated the level of criminal activity that the group's collective character had to undertake for survival. The group chose one of the three cards according to which level of crime they wanted to commit: a low card would be stealing a loaf of bread; a high card, say a 9, would be grand theft or 'coining'.[114] The actors chose their crimes to fit their cards and characters.[115] Each group took it in turn to relate the story of their crime.

After each story had been told, I turned over a card from the remaining pack. If it was the same suit or the same number as their 'crime card', the character had been caught and would be hanged or transported. If it was not the same, they got away with it and earned the sum of the card. Obviously the higher the card they chose the bigger the gamble. The winner was the one who first attained £40 a year.

Arrival in Australia

While Captain Cook 'discovered' Australia in 1770, Aborigines had been living there for 30,000 years.[116] There were approximately 300,000 Aborigines, one to every ten square miles of the continent, when the First Fleet arrived.[117] They were organised into somewhere between 500 to 900 tribes.[118] Originally from Asia, the tribes did not share a common language, the people did not read or write, and they had no discernible kings or gods.[119] The Aborigines were nomadic and lived in harmony with their land. The European concept of property was completely unknown to them; they lived a life of subsistence.

It is difficult to imagine how 'other', how 'alien', Australia was to the transportees from the First Fleet. They faced a completely unknown world. As Robert Hughes points out, Australia seemed further away than the moon – for at least one could see the moon from London.[120] For the convicts, Australia was one huge prison; the unexplored continent became a jail, and around it the Pacific became 'a wall 14,000 miles thick'.[121] The climate, and the animal and plant life, were bewildering.

Many of the convicts were Londoners, so a large part of the problem Governor Phillip faced was that they had few agricultural skills and little ability or inclination to adapt themselves. More or less completely unable to farm or propagate the new land, from lack of skills and knowledge, and being too hungry and hot to work, the white settlers were battling the threat of starvation from as early as 1790. The Second Fleet was slow to arrive and supplies were dwindling; stealing from the colony stores became *instantly* punishable by death.

Governor Phillip was also struggling with the issue of the 'natives'. He had official instructions to be as friendly as possible with them, and to gather scientific knowledge. Phillip was in fact fascinated by the Aborigines, and prevented the convicts from attacking them. In 1789, sixteen convicts set out intent on reprisal when Aborigines injured one of their friends. One convict was killed, and seven injured, but rather than retaliate against the Aborigines, Phillip had the eight unharmed convicts flogged as an example.[122]

Governor Phillip's desire to classify the Aborigines as 'Noble Savages' was doomed to disappointment. Antagonism between the convicts and the Aborigines was not long in arriving. The convicts were outraged by Governor Phillip's liberal treatment and supposed bias towards them. They saw 'the blacks' as primitive, and were glad to encounter people they deemed inferior to themselves. They probably also suffered from jealousy since while the convicts lay on the brink of starvation, the Aborigine population lived in abundance, perfectly accustomed to the flora and fauna of Australia.[123]

In order to reflect this situation in rehearsals – to try to begin to understand how alien the convicts and Aborigines were to each other – I asked any of the actors who spoke another language – French, German, Irish etc. – to play Aborigines, and we improvised an encounter between them and the First Fleet convicts, in which the two groups absolutely failed to understand each other.

Eighteenth-Century Theatre

It is important to understand the context in which the convicts came to Australia, and how they lived. However, *Our Country's Good* is also about staging a play, *The Recruiting Officer*, in 1789. Some knowledge of eighteenth-century theatre and acting is therefore essential to fully comprehending the rehearsal scenes and debates about the theatre in Timberlake's play.

There were two schools of thought on eighteenth-century acting, broadly divided between the 'natural' style pioneered by the actor David Garrick, and the brother and sister, John Philip Kemble and Sarah Siddons, who espoused a new 'classicism'. Both styles of acting were much more physical than we would be used to today, more akin to ballet, say, where formal physical gestures and poses transmit a particular emotion (rage, for example) to the audience.

It appears in the 'First Rehearsal' scene of *Our Country's Good* (Act One, Scene Eleven) that the convicts are conspicuously bad actors, and it is true that a lot of the play's humour derives from their naivety. But the primary mistake made by the most sophisticated convict, Sideway, is the inappropriateness of using the acting style he has observed at Drury Lane for a convict performance in a hut. Acting is simply a language that transmits emotion over distance, and so requires modification within different architectural spaces. Sideway had observed Garrick and Siddons in the huge 2,000-seat Drury Lane Theatre, where a certain emotional flamboyance and energy was required; Garrick's face was said to look twice as old as his body because he 'used it so much'. The only historical description we have of the convict performance of *The Recruiting Officer* estimates the audience at about sixty: about the same size as the Theatre Upstairs at the Royal Court, or a large pub theatre, where acting can clearly be more intimate, and where subtler detail becomes of increased importance.

In Act One, Scene Three ('Punishment') of *Our Country's Good*, the officers discuss a few of the most well-known actors of the time:

> PHILLIP. I never liked Garrick, I always preferred Macklin.
> COLLINS. I'm a Kemble man myself.[124]

DAVID GARRICK (1717–79) was not only an actor, but also a theatre manager, producer and playwright, managing the Theatre Royal, Drury Lane, for twenty-nine years. Garrick shot to fame in 1741 for his naturalistic interpretation of Shakespeare's *Richard III*, which revolutionised acting for ever. As the theatre historian Simon Trussler writes, 'His great strength was apparently in his "turns", or transitions from one mood to another – an ability to modulate the emotions in a subtler manner than the formal style had ever permitted.'[125] Garrick played both Sergeant Kite and Captain Plume from *The Recruiting Officer* over the course of his career. He was afforded a public funeral, and was the first actor buried at Westminster Abbey.

CHARLES MACKLIN (?1699–1797) was a Northern Irish actor and dramatist. Born in Donegal, he found it hard to gain recognition in London with his thick Northern Irish accent and ugly features. In 1741 he performed the part of Shylock in Shakespeare's *The Merchant of Venice*. Running counter to the conventions of the time that treated Shylock as a merely comic figure of fun, he researched into the plight of Italian Jews (much as my own company did for the characters in *Our Country's Good*) and created a realistic, yet tragic portrayal. His Shylock made him famous, and he played the role for the next twenty-five years. He continued to use his research techniques throughout his long life, and passed them on to his many students, including the playwright Samuel Foote (*c*.1721–77).

JOHN PHILIP KEMBLE (1757–1823) was the Manager of Drury Lane from 1788, and of the Theatre Royal, Covent Garden from 1803. Unlike Garrick's 'transitions', Kemble found a consistent through-line in a character: 'Kemble could seize a character by the scruff of its neck, and drag it undeviatingly along its course; he was evidently unmatchable in his generation.'[126] Kemble played Plume in a revival of *The Recruiting Officer*.

> SIDEWAY. Ah, I see ladies approaching: our future
> Woffingtons, Siddons.[127]

PEG WOFFINGTON (*c*.1720–60) was an Irish actress who became the Marilyn Monroe of the eighteenth-century stage. In 1740, she was spotted in Dublin playing Sir Harry Wildair in George Farquhar's successful 1699 play *The Constant Couple*, and moved to London. Sir Harry Wildair is a so-called 'breeches' role – a role in which a woman plays a man, thereby titillating the largely male audience by allowing them to see the actresses' legs, which of course were covered with long skirts when they played women. The same crowd-pleasing formula is used when Silvia dresses up as Jack Wilful in *The Recruiting Officer*.

SARAH SIDDONS (1755–1831) was John Kemble's older sister and appeared at Drury Lane one season before him. She was the most famous actress of her age, most notably dazzling audiences with her psychological portrayal of Lady Macbeth. Trussler nicely describes how she attempted 'to allow her character to emerge from a web of human motives rather than dramatic conventions'.[128] Her immense talents helped make acting a respectable profession for women.

Ralph Clark is referred to as the 'director' in *Our Country's Good*, but this is a plausible anachronism on Timberlake's part. In the late eighteenth century the director's duties were shared among the leading actors, the playwright, the prompter and the theatre managers, and Timberlake has taken some liberties intertwining twentieth-century directing techniques. Ralph coaxes Liz to 'feel' like a rich lady, for example. This is clearly drawn from Stanislavskian acting.[129] Ralph also urges Sideway to be more naturalistic – to which Sideway responds, 'Natural! On the stage! But Mr Clark!'[130]

1980s Britain

'It doesn't matter when a play is set,' claims Wisehammer in Act Two, Scene Seven ('The Meaning of Plays') of *Our Country's Good*. 'It's better if it's set in the past, it's clearer.'[131] While Timberlake's play is set in 1789, she sees it as very much a modern play: 'The thinking I did was about the period I was in when I wrote it.' Timberlake had supplied a precedent in her earlier work for setting modern issues in a past context. Her 1985 play *The Grace of Mary Traverse*, for example, showed the struggle of a young woman in eighteenth-century England to achieve self-realisation in a world where, historically, this was only an option for men, and she had also translated and adapted Ancient Greek plays for modern audiences.

As Timberlake herself explains, 'It bothers me that people feel it all has to be *now* – it has to be journalism rather than imagination, and you have to see things front-on rather than obliquely. History is a great metaphor. *Our Country's Good* is not meant to be a history play about history, it's meant to be a metaphor.'

As previously mentioned, the research conducted during our workshop was thoroughly contemporary – meeting prisoners, discussing the possibilities of redemption through education, and so on. And of course the affirmation of the power of theatre was hugely pertinent in 1988. Under Mrs Thatcher, arts funding was squeezed to a minimum and there was a tangible sense that the theatre community was under very real threat. Indeed, the Royal Court itself was so financially stricken that we were only able to produce about half the amount of work we had achieved fifteen years earlier. And Timberlake suggests another way in which *Our Country's Good* supplied a wider commentary on Thatcherism: 'There was a sense of the devaluation of society – famously "there's no such thing as society" – therefore everybody's on their own, which is what this play does *not* say. It says the opposite: that you *can* form a community.'

ACTIONING

One of the methods of directing I have developed over my career has been 'actioning'. Actioning is a method of analysing and breaking down a script by defining the intentions and tactics taken by a particular character. It is a system pretty well based on Stanislavsky's.

Normally I spend the first two weeks of a rehearsal period sitting around a table with the actors and finding the 'action' for each line in the script. The method works something like this: firstly, break the scene down into units. Each of these units is determined by what the character that runs the scene wants, and this can then be described in a complete sentence.

Let's take Act One, Scene Five of *Our Country's Good* ('An Audition') as an example. Ralph Clark is auditioning Mary Brenham. The first question to ask is: 'Who is running the scene to begin with?' Well, Ralph is obviously trying to, but in fact it is Dabby Bryant who imposes her will more effectively, and so the first unit might therefore be called 'Dabby wants to interest Ralph in Mary' or, more crudely, 'Dabby wants to pimp Mary'.

Then, as a company, we would seek to find a transitive verb that describes each tactic, or change of thought, that goes towards achieving the unit's objective. Consider the following exchange:

> DABBY. You asked to see Mary Brenham, Lieutenant. Here she is.

This is a very direct and bold line. Certainly, Ralph is already aware of Mary from the boat and Dabby has spotted that he fancies her. So we could try the verb 'CONFRONTS' as a suitable description; 'TITILLATES' or 'STIRS' might also work.

> RALPH. Yes – the Governor has asked me to put on a play.
> (To MARY.) You know what a play is?

There may well be two actions to Ralph's line here: the first to Dabby to establish the probity of his motives; and the second to Mary to discover her previous experience. So we could try 'CORRECTS', 'FOCUSES' or 'SETTLES', and then 'QUIZZES'; or maybe if he's aware of Mary's timidity, the second action could be 'CALMS' or 'DRAWS OUT'.

But Dabby still wants to take charge of the scene, and her next action on –

> DABBY. I've seen lots of plays, Lieutenant, so has Mary.

– is 'IMPRESSES'; or if the last three words are interpreted as a separate thought, there might be two actions: perhaps 'IMPRESSES' and 'REASSURES'.

> RALPH. Have you, Brenham?

This is the most direct Ralph has been. The action could be 'DRAWS OUT', but if this has already been used in the scene, a different verb may be required. Perhaps 'CHALLENGES' is too bold, but 'PROBES' might catch it; or, if he believes Dabby, it could be 'ENTHUSES OVER'.

To this question, Mary simply – and according to Timberlake's script '*inaudibly*' – replies 'Yes', which in actioning terms is probably 'PLEASES' since she knows what answer he wants.

> RALPH. Can you remember which plays you've seen?

The transitive verb here could be 'SUSPECTS' – if Ralph thinks she is simply trying to please him, 'FISHES' or 'ENTHUSES' maybe – if he thinks he has already found a willing and keen theatregoer.

Mary replies, 'No.' She knows this is not the answer Ralph wants, but on the other hand, if she says 'Yes', her ignorance is likely to be exposed by Ralph's further questioning. So her action might be 'PREPARES' or 'LEVELS' or even 'WARNS'. ('LEVELS' might still be a bit doubtful, however: it's a metaphor, and it is generally best to avoid those if possible.)

These actioning verbs can be incorporated into Timberlake's play, as follows:

> DABBY. [IMPRESSES] I can't remember what they were called, but I always knew when they were going to end badly. [AMAZES] I knew right from the beginning. [ENGAGES] How does this one end, Lieutenant?

Dabby's analysis may sound naive, but is far from being stupid. As Farquhar himself wrote in one of his essays on playwriting, 'The tragedy of all comedy is that it must end in marriage. The comedy of all tragedy is that it must end in death.' The rules for an eighteenth-century playwright were pretty rigid in terms of genre, so Dabby is simply and sensibly asking what sort of play this is: a comedy or a tragedy.

> RALPH. It ends happily. It's called *The Recruiting Officer*.

Ralph is probably by now growing weary of Dabby's interjections and her determination to run the scene, so his action here is perhaps 'SATISFIES' or 'PLACATES'. But Dabby is unstoppable, and she 'CONFRONTS' Ralph directly:

> DABBY. [CONFRONTS] Mary wants to be in your play,
> Lieutenant, and so do I.

Ralph now attempts to seize the initiative:

> RALPH. [FOCUSES] Do you think you have a talent for
> acting, Brenham?

But Dabby will have none of it:

> DABBY. [DISMISSES] Of course she does, [IMPRESSES] and so
> do I. [CONFRONTS] I want to play Mary's friend.

There are probably simpler ways of actioning Dabby's lines, but these three ('DISMISSES... IMPRESSES... CONFRONTS') seem usefully to define the stages of her thoughts. Her words also probably bring to an end the first of the units we have been looking at ('Dabby wants to interest Ralph in Mary'), and we might call the next unit 'Ralph wants to quieten Dabby' or 'Ralph wants to shut Dabby up'.

> RALPH. Do you know *The Recruiting Officer*, Bryant?

If Ralph is seeking to silence Dabby, his action towards her here might be defined as 'BELITTLES' or 'EXPOSES' – though once again, her theatrical intuition is shrewd and correct: most leading characters in Restoration plays indeed have a 'friend' (or 'confidante') to whom they can reveal their plans. So the better description of Ralph's action here might just as conceivably be 'DRAWS OUT' or 'SUSPECTS'. And Dabby's reply may be actioned as follows:

> DABBY. [IMPRESSES] No, but in all those plays, there's
> always a friend. That's because a girl has to talk to
> someone and she talks to her friend. [PERSUADES *or*
> CONFRONTS] So I'll be Mary's friend.

A new unit will follow on, as Ralph begins to focus on Mary... and so the exercise continues – each time defining the immediate 'action' that motivates a character's words.

STATUS

During rehearsals I also work with the actors on 'status'. Obviously, in *Our Country's Good* the officers are of higher status than the convicts, but among the officers and the convicts there is also a pecking order or hierarchy. The officers' status is determined by rank, with Governor Phillip as the highest status, and Harry Brewer as Provost Marshal the lowest.

One way to introduce a group of actors to 'status' is by playing the following game. Each actor chooses a card from a pack to a value of between 2 and 10 (the aces and face cards are removed). The actors then move around the group, talking and introducing themselves to each other, playing the status of the card they have randomly picked, but without disclosing the number of their card. See if the group can rank themselves in order of hierarchy. Once they've had several goes, change the group into Officers, and then Convicts, and play the game again. Finally, choose the individual characters from the play and 'rate' or evaluate them in terms of their status.

Of course a character's 'status' is always changing within a play. For example, at the start of *Our Country's Good*, Mary probably ranks very lowly in the criminal fraternity but once the production comes nearer to fruition her dedication and acting skills place her very near the top in the acting troupe.

The Convicts

What is the starting point of the convicts' status? There appears to be an inner circle or gang which Liz Morden refers to: 'good crew of rufflers, Kable, Arscott.'[132] The hierarchy might go something like this:

10	KABLE	An offstage character, Ralph has cast him as Captain Plume, so presumably he has a certain charisma among the convicts.

9	LIZ MORDEN	We know she is violent and foul-mouthed, and the other women hate her – Duckling refuses to act with her, and Dabby teases her for not being able to read. However, her violent reputation makes her dangerous and therefore of high status.
8	DABBY BRYANT	She was convicted for 'robbery on the King's Highway' and certainly her extraordinary bravery, organisational ability and leadership was shown in her amazing escape from Sydney.
7	SIDEWAY	A professional pickpocket, his skills would be valued and appreciated by the others.
6	ARSCOTT	The brutalised 'enforcer' of the gang. Never very high in a gang hierarchy.
5	DUCKLING SMITH	Duckling Smith is a former child prostitute and would not rate at all within the convict hierarchy.
4	WISEHAMMER	Not a criminal at all. Those who continually protest their innocence are often despised. He is also Jewish, and so an outcast among the convicts.
3	CAESAR	It's hard to know whether he would have been more abused for being black or for speaking French. Nor does he rate highly as a member of the acting troupe: he is drunk and terrified before the performance.
2	MARY BRENHAM	Young and attractive, she appears to have been pimped by Dabby Bryant who acts as her protector.

There remains Ketch Freeman, who barely rates a 1, so despised is he by the rest of the convicts for taking on the role of hangman. He deliberately seeks a part in the play to humanise himself in the eyes of the women.

At the end of the play when priorities have changed, so too has the hierarchy:

10	MARY BRENHAM	Australia's first leading lady.
10	RALPH CLARK	Although not a convict, Ralph too has risen in the eyes of all. And he is the director.
10	LIZ MORDEN	As the most feared woman, her late conversion to the play is particularly telling and welcomed by the others.
8	SIDEWAY	His enthusiasm for the play makes him of great value.
7	WISEHAMMER	As the writer of the new prologue, Timberlake would not let him be too low in the hierarchy.
7	ARSCOTT	His skills are probably minimal, but his enthusiasm is valuable. He also takes the lead in finding the absconding Caesar.
6	DUCKLING SMITH	She is a reluctant actress, but 'Harry liked to hear me say my lines'.
4	KETCH FREEMAN	He has succeeded in making himself indispensable and has become the essential stage manager figure. His journey from a 1 to a 4 is as significant as any.
3	DABBY BRYANT	She has her mind on more important issues and sees through the heady illusions offered by the play.
1	CAESAR	Drunk, unreliable. Not a welcome figure in any dressing room.

Thus the theatre's ability to effect change in people's lives is shown by the journey of the characters. Charting the change in status of the characters helps us envisage their journey through the play. Obviously the journey for Ralph, Mary and Liz Morden is striking and clear.

The Officers

Most of the officers appear in only one or two scenes. But the officers that appear throughout *Our Country's Good* also have a journey. As noted above, Ralph goes from being thought of as 'a fluter, a mollie… a prissy cove, a girl!' by the convicts to being respected and championed by them, a status of 7. Presumably his status has also risen in the eyes of Governor Phillip, Davy Collins and the other officers, if not Robbie Ross.

Ross remains resolutely against the play from start to finish. He starts as a high-status character, an 8, given his rank as a Major who holds the power of promotion in his hands. But the success of the play and its positive effect on the convicts surely serves to undermine him in the eyes of his fellow officers. This can be seen in the change in Captain Jemmy Campbell, who began by agreeing with everything Ross uttered. By Act Two, Scene Ten ('The Question of Liz'), even he has been changed by the play: 'Good scene that, very funny, hah,' he comments, instead of sporting an indistinguishable and incomprehensible broth of Caledonian bile. This limited ability to think for himself probably improves his status in the eyes of the other officers.

Davy Collins, also a status of 8, begins in Act One, Scene Three ('Punishment') by mocking Phillip's interest in educating the convicts, preferring to focus on their punishment. But by Act Two, Scene Ten ('The Question of Liz') he displays some humanity towards Liz Morden, even if it is in the guise of justice. His status as Advocate General will have risen in the eyes of the convicts, who will appreciate that Liz can act in the play, and of Governor Phillip, who would appreciate his fairness.

Governor Phillip, of course, also has a journey, but has a status of 10. He goes from believing in the idea of reforming the convicts through education and ends with his theory being proven. While he is Governor from the beginning, he was viewed with some derision by the officers for his liberal view of the convicts and by the convicts themselves for his neutrality with the Aborigines. By the end, more of the officers are on his side, and of course the convicts will be immensely grateful for the privileges he has afforded them.

CARDS

We have seen how the use of playing cards can provide a way in to understanding status. Cards can also determine the strength of a character's feelings. The most pertinent example of this in *Our Country's Good* is in Act One, Scene Six ('The Authorities Discuss the Merits of the Theatre'). If we say a black card determines opposition to Ralph's play and red support for it, and if the number on the card determines the strength of that feeling, so a 2 is not strong and a 10 is extremely passionate, we can rank the officers something like this:

Red		Black	
10	RALPH CLARK	10	ROBBIE ROSS
9	GOVERNOR PHILLIP	8	JEMMY CAMPBELL
6	GEORGE JOHNSTON	7	WILLIAM FADDY
4	DAVY COLLINS	3	REVEREND JOHNSON
		3	WATKIN TENCH
		2	WILLIAM DAWES

Try rehearsing the scene with these cards in mind and see if it helps clarify the intensity of support and opposition for the play, and therefore the dynamics of this scene. We can see from this table that although there are six people against the play and four people for it, the highest-status person – Governor Phillip – is a red 9, and the most vehement opponent is Robbie Ross, who is despised by most of his fellow officers. Three of the people against the play are 3s and a 2, so they are not really bothered either way. The outcome of the scene becomes clear from this simple analysis.

However, in order to connect fully with the ideas in the scene, it can help to bring it closer to home. In rehearsal, I temporarily abandoned Australia and asked the actors to be citizens of Shrewsbury – the town where *The Recruiting Officer* is set – but of course you could choose your home town. The scenario I presented was that there was no professional theatre within thirty miles of the town: should the council fund a local amateur dramatic society? The actors picked cards at random, and took turns to sit on a chair in front of the group, and express their opinions. I found my actors reconnected with their amateur origins and a lively debate ensued. Ron Cook, the actor who played Governor Phillip, drew a black 4 and argued that the local angling club needed the money more to help clean up the river, Shrewsbury's famous landmark; Lesley Sharp, who played Mary Brenham, fortuitously drew a high red and memorably expressed her heartfelt joy of being part of the Shrewsbury Players.

Jim Broadbent (as Harry Brewer) having nightmares in Act Two, Scene Three: 'Harry Brewer Sees the Dead'.

Staging the Play

When *Our Country's Good* was being written in 1988, the Royal Court had a tiny budget and so the design of the play was intended to be simple and minimal. At the same time, Timberlake is not a fan of big sets, so she envisaged it as very bare, with few set changes. Any play with twenty-two scenes has to be quick and economical in moving from scene to scene, and requires an overall scenic image that relates to the whole play.

Because of the number of scenes and changes of location, and because *Our Country's Good* is driven by the text, it is advisable to have a simple design concept. There are few sound cues in the play and not too many props; but the mood of the scenes – from the desperation on the convict ship, via the punishing and dazzling heat of Australia, to the intimacy of the tents – can be conveyed with a skilful use of lighting.

Our Country's Good is not a naturalistic play, and does not attempt to convey 'a slice of life' from the first few months of the penal colony in Sydney. As Timberlake has stressed, it is a metaphor for the power of theatre to educate and reform. Productions of *Our Country's Good* have been set in locations as varied as Guantanamo Bay and disused prisons around the UK, and Timberlake remains very supportive of finding new metaphors for the work.

In this section I shall outline some of the design choices made in the original Royal Court production and the 1998 Young Vic revival. Then I shall go through each scene, looking at the specific requirements.

SET

For the initial production in 1988, the designer, Peter Hartwell, provided a backdrop that owed a bit to the pictures of Sidney Nolan (1917–92), one of Australia's most influential painters. In Australia, trees grow rather further apart than in England so they can maximise any moisture from the earth; early convict artists mistakenly depicted the landscape as English parkland because those were the visual terms of reference they had. By contrast, Sidney Nolan can depicts a tree with a single stroke through the oil paint.

The furniture was portable: a wooden chair with arms for the Governor; a folding table used by officers in the field; and a number of other stools and chairs. It all had a very temporary feel to it, as though the protagonists were pitching camp rather than making a home.

In the 1998 revival, the designer Julian McGowan and I decided upon a large wooden raft that was hung by chains from the beams of the Young Vic, as the main visual image. This structure was strong enough to bear the weight of the whole cast. In the opening scene, the convicts sat on it and it moved under them like a ship, rocking from side to side. It was also vivid for the other waterborne scene, Act One, Scene Seven ('Harry and Duckling Go Rowing'), in which Harry and Duckling sat opposite each other, at either end of the raft. Harry used two wooden oars, held in place with rowlocks. The raft swung from side to side, and Harry rowed the oars in tandem. In Act Two, Scene One ('Visiting Hours'), it was hoisted up to make a low, invasive ceiling for the prison; and in the officers' scenes it served as a low dais for the Governor's chair.

LIGHTING AND SOUND

The arrival in Sydney, in Act One, Scene Two ('A Lone Aboriginal Australian Describes the Arrival of the First Convict Fleet in Botany Bay on January 20, 1788'), is an opportunity for an explosion of light and sound. Hughes reckons that several dozen kinds of indigenous birds – parakeets, corellas and cockatoos – that breed in the bush around Sydney Harbour must have given voice as the ship dropped anchor. The intense Australian light must have stunned the convicts who had been kept largely below decks with no light for seven months.

Both productions ended with the triumphant sound of Beethoven's *Fifth Symphony*, drowning the recruiting sergeant's opening speech. This is more than slightly anachronistic, since it dates from 1808, but no matter, it provided a rousing and enthralling ending to the play.

PROPS

The final scene enabled us to accumulate props, costumes and primitive pots of make-up on stage, and the same half-curtain used in the first production was also utilised at the end of the revival. We used paintings by Rowlandson (1756–1827) and Hogarth (1697–1764) as research. The Hogarth painting *Strolling Actors Dressing in a Barn* informed the final scene, with the backstage actors peering through the chinks in the curtain at their onstage colleagues.

COSTUME

One of the gripes of the historical officers was that their uniforms faded so significantly in the harsh sunlight of Sydney, and their boots also became so dilapidated, that they were soon indistinguishable from the convicts. This was mirrored in both productions.

There is always a Dick Whittington moment in eighteenth-century plays when actors don wigs or tricorne hats for the first time and the whole thing slides inexorably towards pantomime. We took advantage of this. In Act One, Scene Six ('The Authorities Discuss the Merits of the Theatre'), all the women in the company become male officers. At this point they donned huge wigs that looked like dead spaniels perched on their heads. Since they changed in front of the audience, and there was little attempt to disguise the fact that they were women playing men, it provided a Brechtian moment by acknowledging that we were witnessing a play.

As already mentioned, the officers' clothes deteriorated so they felt no better dressed than the convicts. But of course the convicts were even more dishevelled. Before the voyage to Australia, the male convicts were stripped of their clothes, which were sold to clothes merchants. They were provisioned with a coarse shirt, canvas trousers, a grey jacket and ill-fitting shoes.[133] The women sailed in what they were wearing, which they had already worn for several months on board a hulk. Governor Phillip reported that the state of the women embarking on the convict ship, the *Lady Penrhyn*, was an outrage: 'Tho' almost naked, and so very filthy, that nothing but clothing them could have prevented them from perishing.'[134]

The saltwater, vermin and filth on the voyage destroyed the convicts' clothes, which they didn't get to change, whether when soaked by the Atlantic or covered in the grime of the hold. By the time the First Fleet reached Rio, the convicts' clothes were disintegrating. Governor Phillip bought a hundred sacks of tapioca, as the strong Russian burlap material could make new clothes for the convicts, 'many of whom are nearly naked'.[135]

Interestingly, Linda Bassett, who played Liz Morden, notes the changes between the convict costumes and the costumes they would have worn in *The Recruiting Officer* as mirroring the journeys of the characters: 'In "Visiting Hours", she says she has a big collar, which I chose to have because I wanted to remind people that I was going to be hanged, and Peter Hartwell made me a beautiful little necklace to wear as Melinda; so what was around my neck became part of the story.'

Act One

Scene One: The Voyage Out

CHARACTERS	The convicts, Ralph Clark.
LIGHTING	The first scene takes place in two locations. The stage directions describe '*The hold... The convicts huddle together in the semi-darkness.*' Meanwhile, Sideway is being flogged on deck. Fortunately for a lighting designer, it is night, and so darkness prevails.
SOUND	The whip on Sideway's naked back. Water sloshing against the ship. Creaks.
PROPS	The play begins with a flogging. How can you stage it realistically without harming the actor? We used some form of prosthetic back which the actor playing Sideway wore like a waistcoat – but maybe there are equally dramatic ways of doing it.
COSTUME	It is sometime during the First Fleet's voyage to Australia. The convicts may be barely clothed in their London attire, or perhaps they have been fitted out with sack-cloth. The officers' clothes may still be fairly fresh, although how clean can one be on an eighteenth-century convict ship?

Scene Two: A Lone Aboriginal Australian Describes the Arrival of the First Convict Fleet in Botany Bay on January 20, 1788

CHARACTERS	The Aborigine.
LIGHTING	The Aborigine is watching from Sydney. The contrast between the light in the hold of the convict ship and the Australian summer should be dramatic.
SOUND	Native birds and wildlife.
COSTUME	The officers in *The Playmaker* are obsessed by the fish-oil with which the Aborigines coat

themselves as protection from insects. (Maybe this would be a step too far for an actor?)

Scene Three: Punishment

CHARACTERS   Governor Arthur Phillip, Davy Collins, Watkin Tench, Harry Brewer.

LIGHTING   The men are outdoors, shooting birds in Sydney Cove. It is light and bright: a punishingly hot Australian summer.

SOUND   Gun shots. Native Australian birds and wildlife.

PROPS   There is only one gun, which is loaded and carried by Harry. He passes it to the officer who wishes to take a shot. Remember: gunpowder was precious.

Scene Four: The Loneliness of Men

CHARACTERS   Ralph Clark, Harry Brewer.

LIGHTING   It is Ralph Clark's tent, the first time we go inside on dry land, though as it is a tent we should still sense the outdoors. Ralph has a candle burning – Harry enters because he can see the light from the tent.

PROPS   Ralph's journal, and a quill and ink for writing. A candle and something to light it with.

Scene Five: An Audition

CHARACTERS   Ralph Clark, Meg Long, Sideway, Dabby, Mary, Liz.

LIGHTING   Outdoors. Some time has passed as the colony must be settled enough for Governor Phillip to have thought about doing a play. A little less hot.

PROPS   A copy of *The Recruiting Officer*.

COSTUME   Ralph needs to have a handkerchief that Sideway can steal. Meg Long, aka 'shitty Meg', is extra dirty. Sideway, as a relatively up-market pickpocket, may have slightly more refined clothes than the other convicts. Mary is a young, shy girl of nineteen, whereas Dabby is a mother and the wife of a fisherman – she lives on the 'good side' of the settlement, so could be slightly better dressed.

Scene Six: The Authorities Discuss the Merits of the Theatre

Note: An Officers' Mess is a relatively informal space within a very hierarchical society. The Governor General is referred to as 'Sir' not 'Your Excellency', while he calls the officers by their Christian names rather than 'Major Ross' or 'Lieutenant Clark'.

CHARACTERS   Governor Phillip, Ross, Collins, Tench, Campbell, Reverend Johnson, George Johnston, Dawes, Ralph, Faddy.

LIGHTING   Indoors, late at night. Candlelight.

PROPS   A table. Chairs. Jugs for drinking.

Scene Seven: Harry and Duckling Go Rowing

CHARACTERS   Harry, Duckling.

LIGHTING   Harry and Duckling are on a rowing boat in Sydney Cove. Daylight, a sense of water.

SOUND   Rowing in water. Sydney Cove is a small bay.

PROPS   This all depends on how you decide to stage the rowing scene (see p. 95).

Scene Eight: The Women Learn Their Lines

CHARACTERS   Mary, Dabby, Liz, Ketch.

LIGHTING   Outdoors.

PROPS   A copy of *The Recruiting Officer*.

COSTUME   The stage directions tell us, 'DABBY *begins to lift*
             MARY*'s skirt to reveal a tattoo high up on the inner*
             thigh.' The tattoo could be visible in an intimate
             theatre.

Scene Nine: Ralph Clark Tries to Kiss His Dear Wife's Picture

CHARACTERS   Ralph, Ketch.

LIGHTING   Ralph's tent, midnight. Dead of night outside.
             Candlelight in the tent.

PROPS   Ralph's journal. A Bible. A candle and some-
             thing to light it with. His dear wife's picture –
             a miniature portrait with a hinged glass lid (see
             p. 45).

COSTUME   Ralph is wearing a watch – not a wristwatch
             (since these were twentieth-century inventions),
             but a 'pocket watch', attached to a chain and
             worn in the waistcoat.

Scene Ten: John Wisehammer and Mary Brenham Exchange
Words

CHARACTERS   Wisehammer, Mary.

LIGHTING   Outdoors. Bright afternoon light.

PROPS   A copy of *The Recruiting Officer*. A book or sheaf
             of paper for Mary to copy it into. A quill and ink
             for writing. Wisehammer is carrying bricks.

Scene Eleven: The First Rehearsal

CHARACTERS   Ralph, Sideway, Wisehammer, Mary, Liz,
             Dabby, Duckling, Ketch, Caesar, Ross,
             Campbell.

LIGHTING   Outdoors. Afternoon. Perhaps a little less bright
             than the previous scene – a sense of foreboding.

PROPS   A copy of *The Recruiting Officer* for Ralph, and
              one for Mary. A piece of wood for Duckling to
              give to Liz – playing Melinda – as a fan.

Act Two

Scene One: Visiting Hours

CHARACTERS   Liz, Wisehammer, Arscott, Caesar, Sideway,
              Mary, Duckling.

LIGHTING   In a prison. Dark and dank.

PROPS   Liz, Wisehammer, Arscott and Caesar are in
              chains. Mary has a copy of *The Recruiting Offi-
              cer*, Duckling brings Melinda's fan, or
              something representing it.

Scene Two: His Excellency Exhorts Ralph

CHARACTERS   Governor Phillip, Ralph.

LIGHTING   Inside a tent, during the day.

PROPS   Phillip's tent will be more comfortable and well-
              equipped than Ralph's. Phillip's status could be
              displayed visually. They could be seated. Phillip
              might be on a small rostrum.

Scene Three: Harry Brewer Sees the Dead

CHARACTERS   Harry, Duckling.

LIGHTING   Inside Harry's tent at night.

PROPS   A bottle of rum. Harry's tent would be similar
              to Ralph's, perhaps even more basic. Harry has
              a chipped mug.

Scene Four: The Aborigine Muses on the Nature of Dreams

CHARACTERS   The Aborigine.

SOUND   Didgeridoo music behind.

Scene Five: The Second Rehearsal

CHARACTERS Ralph, Mary, Sideway, Ross, Campbell, Caesar, Liz, Wisehammer; Arscott (offstage).

LIGHTING Outdoors. Daytime.

PROPS Ralph has a copy of *The Recruiting Officer*.

COSTUME Liz, Caesar and Wisehammer are still in chains. Campbell unchains Wisehammer and Caesar. Sideway must remove his shirt and display his scarred back from the flogging in scene one – he was flogged three hundred times, so his back is severely scarred and corrugated.

Scene Six: The Science of Hanging

CHARACTERS Liz, Ketch, Harry.

LIGHTING Outdoors. Daytime.

PROPS Liz is sitting on something. Ketch is measuring her with a piece of knotted rope.

Scene Seven: The Meaning of Plays

CHARACTERS The Aborigine, Mary, Ralph, Dabby, Wisehammer, Arscott.

LIGHTING Outdoors. Daytime.

PROPS Ralph has a copy of *The Recruiting Officer*. A piece of paper with Wisehammer's prologue written on it.

Scene Eight: Duckling Makes Vows

CHARACTERS Harry, Duckling.

LIGHTING Harry's tent, night.

Scene Nine: A Love Scene

CHARACTERS Mary, Ralph.

LIGHTING The beach. Night. Moonlight.

SOUND The sound of the sea.

COSTUME Mary and Ralph undress one another.

Scene Ten: The Question of Liz

CHARACTERS Liz, Governor Phillip, Collins, Ralph, Ross, Campbell.

LIGHTING Indoors. Daytime.

PROPS Collins could stand at a lectern. He may have a judge's gavel.

COSTUME A judge's wig for Collins. Liz is chained at the wrists.

Scene Eleven: Backstage

CHARACTERS The Aborigine, the convicts and Ralph.

LIGHTING Night. Backstage at a makeshift theatre in a tent. The convicts are probably behind a curtain.

SOUND The play ends to the sound of Beethoven's triumphant *Fifth Symphony*. Laughter and applause as Arscott and Caesar go on stage.

PROPS An orange for Mary to give to Duckling. Salt for Sideway to distribute. A piece of paper with Wisehammer's prologue written on it. A drum for Caesar's entrance on stage. The props used by the convicts in their production of *The Recruiting Officer* are not specified in the text: use the text of *The Recruiting Officer* for ideas as to what they might have had. Remember they wouldn't have had much by way of theatrical props in the new penal colony, so they must be things that could have been easily made or borrowed from the officers. There would be a few pots of stage make-up for the actors to share.

COSTUME   The Aborigine has small-pox pustules on his skin. The convicts will be in their costumes for their parts in *The Recruiting Officer*: Mary as Silvia (a well-to-do country girl); Liz as Melinda (a newly rich heiress); Ralph as Plume would probably wear his own officer's uniform; Arscott as Kite and Wisehammer as Brazen (recruiting officers) would have borrowed their costumes from the officers; Ketch as Justice Balance would also have an official uniform; Sideway as Worthy (a gentleman of Shropshire) may have borrowed clothes from an officer; Dabby as Rose (a country girl) would wear basic clothes, perhaps her own; Duckling as Lucy (Melinda's maid) would have a rich woman's-maid's outfit, possibly made for her.

A FINAL NOTE

The last scene should capture the excitement and pleasurable anticipation of the imminent performance. It encapsulates Timberlake's central thesis of the uplifting power of drama even under the most adverse of circumstances. The journey of the play is from a brutal beating to Mary Brenham's 'I love this'.

Endnotes

1. Playwrights today are usually rewarded with a percentage (around ten per cent) of box-office takings. In the early eighteenth century a playwright's income was from 'benefit performances' when they received most of the box-office income for that night. Benefits were given on the third night of a run, the sixth, the ninth and so on, though most plays ran for only a few nights because the theatregoing population of London was small. *The Recruiting Officer* played for eight performances in April 1706; the prudent management took it out of the repertoire rather than give Farquhar a third benefit. Over the next twenty years the play enjoyed 124 performances.

2. Farquhar does not specify the time of year, but it's clearly a few months after the Battle of Blenheim, which took place on 13 August. Recruiting drives traditionally took place in the autumn.

3. George Farquhar, *The Recruiting Officer*, edited by Simon Trussler (Nick Hern Books: London, 1997), p. 18.

4. Timberlake Wertenbaker, *Our Country's Good*, with commentary and notes by Bill Naismith (Methuen Drama: London, 2006), p. 22.

5. Farquhar, *The Recruiting Officer*, p. 51.

6. Wertenbaker, *Our Country's Good*, p. 17.

7. *Ibid.*, p. 18.

8. Farquhar, *The Recruiting Officer*, p. xiii.

9. Thomas Keneally, *The Playmaker* (Sceptre: London, 1987), p. 72.

10. Wertenbaker, *Our Country's Good*, p. 65.

11. *Ibid.*, p. 69.

12. *Ibid.*, p. 75.

13. *Ibid.*, p. 4.

14. *Ibid.*, p. 78.

15. *Ibid.*, p. 59.

16. *Ibid.*, p. 57.

17. *Ibid.*, p. 18.

18. *Ibid.*, p. 64.

19. Robert Hughes, *The Fatal Shore* (Vintage: London, 1987), p. 95.

20. Billy Reid, Letter to Timberlake Wertenbaker, 8 November 1990, in Wertenbaker, *Our Country's Good*, p. lix.

21. Hughes, *The Fatal Shore*, p. 118.

22. *Ibid.*, p. 122.

23. *Ibid.*, p. 128.

24. Keneally, *The Playmaker*, p. 47–8.

25. Wertenbaker, *Our Country's Good*, p. 5.

26. *Ibid.*, p. 80.

27. Hughes, *The Fatal Shore*, p. 77.
28. Judith Cook, *To Brave Every Danger: The Epic Life of Mary Bryant of Fowey* (Truran Books: Cornwall, 2003), p. 239.
29. *Ibid.*, pp. 239–40.
30. *Ibid.*, p. 239.
31. Wertenbaker, *Our Country's Good*, p. 4.
32. *Ibid.*, p. 4.
33. *Ibid.*, p. 22.
34. Keneally, *The Playmaker*, p. 134.
35. *Ibid.*, p. 45.
36. Wertenbaker, *Our Country's Good*, p. 19.
37. Cook, *To Brave Every Danger*, p. 124.
38. Hughes, *The Fatal Shore*, p. 249.
39. Keneally, *The Playmaker*, p. 51.
40. Hughes, *The Fatal Shore*, p. 248.
41. *Ibid.*, p. 249.
42. Hughes, *The Fatal Shore*, p. 250.
43. *Ibid.*, p. 250.
44. Wertenbaker, *Our Country's Good*, p. 6.
45. *Ibid.*, p. 9.
46. *Ibid.*, pp. 22–3.
47. *Ibid.*, p. 60.
48. *Ibid.*, p. 72.
49. *Ibid.*, p. 78.
50. *Ibid.*, p. 79.
51. *Ibid.*, p. 90.
52. Keneally, *The Playmaker*, p. 360.
53. *Ibid.*, p. 40.
54. Wertenbaker, *Our Country's Good*, p. 74.
55. Hughes, *The Fatal Shore*, p. 32.
56. Keneally, *The Playmaker*, p. 361.
57. *Ibid.*, p. 13.
58. *Ibid.*, p. 65.
59. *Ibid.*, p. 66.
60. An 'emancipist' was a convict who had been given a pardon; they were free to live in Australia and own land, but were not allowed to leave the colony.
61. Cook, *To Brave Every Danger*, p. 127.
62. Hughes, *The Fatal Shore*, p. 72.
63. Cook, *To Brave Every Danger*, p. 127.
64. Keneally, *The Playmaker*, p. 361.
65. *Ibid.*, p. 278.
66. *Ibid.*, p. 321.
67. Cook, *To Brave Every Danger*, p. 241.
68. Wertenbaker, *Our Country's Good*, p. 1.
69. *Ibid.*, p. 30.
70. *Ibid.*, p. 31.
71. *Ibid.*, p. 56.

72. *Ibid.*, p. 70.
73. *Ibid.*, p. 85.
74. *Ibid.*, p. 30.
75. *Ibid.*, p. 85.
76. Keneally, *The Playmaker*, p. 360.
77. Wertenbaker, *Our Country's Good*, p. 83.
78. Joe White is a remarkable man. He had been a prisoner in Wormwood Scrubs and an actor in the production of *A Love of a Good Man* that we saw. On his release he became my assistant, and his advice and acquaintance with imprisonment were seminal.
79. Keneally, *The Playmaker*, p. 159.
80. Hughes, *The Fatal Shore*, p. 11.
81. Keneally, *The Playmaker*, p. 37.
82. Hughes, *The Fatal Shore*, p. 25.
83. *Ibid.*, pp. 25–6.
84. *Ibid.*, p. 24.
85. *Ibid.*, p. 27.
86. *Ibid.*, p. 28.
87. *Ibid.*, p. 29.
88. *Ibid.*, p. 35.
89. *Ibid.*, p. 35.
90. Wertenbaker, *Our Country's Good*, p. 2.
91. John Locke, *Some Thoughts Concerning Education*, ed. John W. Yolton and Jean S. Yolton (Clarendon Press: Oxford, 1990), p. 83.
92. Wertenbaker, *Our Country's Good*, p. 3.
93. Hughes, *The Fatal Shore*, p. 31.
94. *Ibid.*, p. 31.
95. Wertenbaker, *Our Country's Good*, p. 4.
96. Cook, *To Brave Every Danger*, pp. 74–5.
97. Hughes, *The Fatal Shore*, p. 41.
98. It turned out that exporting Norfolk Island pine to Europe proved too costly to get off the ground. The flax industry was also a non-starter as the convicts lacked the skills and equipment to make anything of it. What was supposed to have been a self-supporting colony with an export economy, turned out to be wholly dependent on supplies from half-a-world away in Britain for several precarious years.
99. Hughes, *The Fatal Shore*, p. 2.
100. *Ibid.*, p. 145.
101. *Ibid.*, p. 105.
102. Short solid bolts between the ankles, about nine inches long, that incapacitated the wearer.
103. Hughes, *The Fatal Shore*, p. 145.
104. *Ibid.*, p. 145.
105. *Ibid.*, pp. 145–6.
106. *Ibid.*, p. 147.
107. *Ibid.*, p. 148.
108. *Ibid.*, p. 69.

109. *Ibid.*, p. 156.
110. Men who were familiar with sailing, conscripted by force into the navy. It was the only form of conscription in the British armed forces, and was much opposed.
111. Hughes, *The Fatal Shore*, p. 79.
112. Wertenbaker, *Our Country's Good*, p. 53.
113. *Ibid.*, p. 30.
114. Forging currency.
115. Kings and Queens were trump cards. A King symbolised a 'King's Pardon', which could be used as a reprieve if a character was condemned to death. (This was the equivalent of a local vicar or other person of high standing supplying a character reference.) A Queen meant you were pregnant (male characters could swap or sell this card). If caught you could use these cards to change your sentence from transportation into imprisonment, or from hanging to transportation.
116. Hughes, *The Fatal Shore*, p. 8.
117. *Ibid.*, p. 9.
118. *Ibid.*, p. 9.
119. *Ibid.*, p. 9.
120. *Ibid.*, p. 77.
121. *Ibid.*, p. 1.
122. *Ibid.*, p. 94.
123. *Ibid.*, p. 7.
124. Wertenbaker, *Our Country's Good*, p. 5.
125. Simon Trussler, *The Cambridge Illustrated History of British Theatre* (Cambridge University Press: Cambridge, 2000), p. 176.
126. *Ibid.*, p. 207.
127. Wertenbaker, *Our Country's Good*, p. 12.
128. Trussler, *The Cambridge Illustrated History of British Theatre*, p. 208.
129. Konstantin Stanislavsky (1863–1938) was a Russian actor and theatre director who pioneered a 'naturalistic' form of acting, encouraging his actors to use 'emotion memory' to find the motives and intentions for their characters' actions. For him, actors should 'live the part' – a huge change from the stylised acting that preceded him.
130. Wertenbaker, *Our Country's Good*, p. 45.
131. *Ibid.*, p. 74.
132. *Ibid.*, p. 54.
133. Hughes, *The Fatal Shore*, p. 139.
134. *Ibid.*, p. 71.
135. *Ibid.*, p. 80.

Bibliography

Cook, Judith, *To Brave Every Danger: The Epic Life of Mary Bryant of Fowey* (Truran Books: Cornwall, 2003)

Farquhar, George, *The Recruiting Officer*, edited and introduced by Simon Trussler (Nick Hern Books: London, 1997)

Grenville, Kate, *The Secret River* (Canongate Books: Edinburgh, 2006)

————, *The Lieutenant* (Canongate Books: Edinburgh, 2009)

Hughes, Robert, *The Fatal Shore* (Vintage: London, 1987)

Keneally, Thomas, *The Playmaker* (Sceptre: London, 1987)

Locke, John, *Some Thoughts Concerning Education*, ed. John W. Yolton and Jean S. Yolton (Clarendon Press: Oxford, 1990)

Stafford-Clark, Max, *Letters to George: The Account of a Rehearsal* (Nick Hern Books: London, 1989)

Stafford-Clark, Max, and Phillip Roberts, *Taking Stock: The Theatre of Max Stafford-Clark* (Nick Hern Books: London, 2007)

Trussler, Simon, *The Cambridge Illustrated History of British Theatre* (Cambridge University Press: Cambridge, 2000)

Wertenbaker, Timberlake, *Our Country's Good*, with commentary and notes by Bill Naismith (Methuen Drama: London, 2006)

Willey, Keith, *When the Sky Fell Down: The Destruction of the Tribes of the Sydney Region 1788–1850s* (Collins: Sydney, 1979; reprinted 1985)

PAGE TO STAGE

Written by established theatre professionals, the volumes in the *Page to Stage* series offer highly accessible guides to the world's best-known plays – from an essentially theatrical perspective.

Unlike fiction and poetry, the natural habitat of the play is not the printed page but the living stage. It is therefore often difficult, when reading a play on the page, to grasp how much the staging can release and enhance its true meaning.

The purpose of this series, *Page to Stage*, is to bring this theatrical perspective into the picture – and apply it to some of the best-known, most performed and most studied plays in our literature. Moreover, the authors of these guides are not only well-known theatre practitioners but also established writers, giving them an unrivalled insight and authority.

TITLES IN THE PAGE TO STAGE SERIES

Michael Pennington: Chekhov's *Three Sisters*

Stephen Unwin: Ibsen's *A Doll's House*

Max Stafford-Clark with Maeve McKeown:
Timberlake Wertenbaker's *Our Country's Good*